"I found Greg Ogden when I was searching for call to raise up disciples in a maximum securi *pleship* has been our guidebook as God has created hot houses of the Holy Spirit' throughout our prison. Hundreds of men's lives have been and continue to be changed through the path shown in this book."

Craig Brubaker, volunteer chaplain, Texas Department of Criminal Justice

"*Transforming Discipleship* is truly transforming. This book brings out the importance of discipleship and illustrates the processes of healthy, reproducible methods of disciple making. Deep biblical insight compels and challenges us to go back to the practice Jesus established."

Pradeep Jha, president, Tabernacle Ministries

"No one gets the why and how of transforming ordinary people into extraordinary disciples like Greg Ogden does. As someone who worked alongside of him for ten years, I know that disciple making isn't a theory for Greg, but a way of life. In this revised edition of his landmark book, Greg offers individuals and churches an invaluable manual for shaping circles and cultures that are truly transformative in the way that Jesus and Paul originally had in mind."

Daniel Meyer, senior pastor, Christ Church of Oak Brook, author of *Witness Essentials*, coauthor of *Leadership Essentials*

"No book has influenced my understanding of discipleship group dynamics and multiplication more than *Transforming Discipleship*. Through years of research, field-testing, group implementation, and individual feedback, Greg offers a proven, timeless method for making disciples who will make even more disciples. Every pastor, church leader, and follower of Christ should read this book and apply the principles it teaches."

Robby Gallaty, pastor, Long Hollow Baptist Church, author of *Rediscovering Discipleship*

"Not only inspiring but compelling for all Christian leaders who are desperately searching for answers to the urgent question of how we can create a reproducible hothouse for discipleship and genuine spiritual transformation. If I could only have room for a handful of discipleship books on my shelf, this would definitely be one of them! It's a book I will keep reading over and over to mine its contents fully. Kudos to you, Greg, for writing an even deeper and richer next edition!"

Mary Schaller, president, Q Place, author of *The 9 Arts of Spiritual Conversations*

"Greg has relentlessly grappled with what it means to be Jesus' disciple and what it means to obey Jesus' command to 'make disciples of all nations.' This book is the fruit of that grappling. And, oh, what delicious fruit it is! What Greg writes is simultaneously convicting (the fact is, we are not doing the work) and encouraging (actually, if we just follow the Master's method, we can do the work!).

Darrell W. Johnson, director, Centre of Preaching, Carey Theological College, Vancouver, author of *The Glory of Preaching*

"This is one of the foremost books written on biblical discipleship (practically, philosophically, and theologically) in the last fifty years! Why? It is founded on God's Word, with a extensive focus on how Jesus, the ultimate disciple maker, equipped his apostles to multiply and change the world! Greg writes brilliantly and clearly and also shares from his own experiences in pouring his life into a few. If you are curious or have a passion to impact others for God's glory by following Jesus' method of investing in a few, read this book."

Monte Starkes, director, Life on Life and Global Outreach, Perimeter Church

"Greg Ogden's lifelong passion for growing true disciples culminates in his outstanding *Transforming Discipleship*. In our day, in which congregations know their church programs are no longer as fruitful in growing disciples, Greg gives a solid foundation for developing discipleship based on the ministry of Jesus. He offers wonderful counsel in the use of what he calls 'microgroups,' a church-based strategy for making disciples. I can't wait to put this book into the hands of countless pastors and congregations looking for biblically grounded practices that actually grow disciples."

E. Stanley Ott, founder and president, Vital Churches Institute

"Greg's genius in *Transforming Discipleship* is that he calls the church back to making disciples a few at a time. Jesus chose twelve men to disciple—three in particular. Why, then, don't we see discipleship groups of three and four filling our churches and serving in our communities? Greg addresses this problem and lays out a brilliantly biblical solution: start making disciples a few at a time! It's a must-read for every pastor—indeed for all followers of Christ. The revised and expanded edition is fantastic—especially chapter ten, in which Greg emphasizes the importance of proclaiming a gospel that leads to discipleship."

Ben Sobels, senior pastor, Cypress Community Church, Salinas, California

"Greg Ogden nails it again. This revised and expanded version of his how-to and why-to disciple-making manifesto will continue to be a real asset to the modern church. The lost art of disciple making requires this fresh appraisal and application for the current generation in light of the extensive popularity of program-driven growth strategies. Greg's book is a well-balanced, timely, and practical tool for pastors and lay leaders alike who want to embrace both the message and the method of Jesus Christ for reaching the world through intentional multiplication."

Christopher Moody, pastor, professor, Liberty University School of Divinity

"This book launched a transformational revitalization of our church. As scores of our people began to join quads and triads focused on becoming more like Jesus and learning how to follow Christ's last command, we found a new, deep satisfaction. We had discovered Christ's real intention for his followers. We had spent more than twenty-five years trying to build a successful church. But Jesus never told us to go into all the world and build churches. He told us to go and make disciples and that he would build his church. This is a dangerous book. It may require you to change how you do church."

Ralph Rittenhouse, retired pastor of Camarillo Community Church

TRANSFORMING

DISCIPLESHIP

Making Disciples a Few at a Time

REVISED AND EXPANDED

Greg Ogden

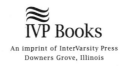

IVP Books

An imprint of InterVarsity Press
Downers Grove, Illinois

InterVarsity Press
P.O. Box 1400, Downers Grove, IL 60515-1426
ivpress.com
email@ivpress.com

InterVarsity Press® is the book-publishing division of InterVarsity Christian Fellowship/USA®, a movement of
students and faculty active on campus at hundreds of universities, colleges and schools of nursing in the United States of
America, and a member movement of the International Fellowship of Evangelical Students. For information about
local and regional activities, visit intervarsity.org.

Scripture quotations, unless otherwise noted, are from the New Revised Standard Version of the Bible, copyright 1989
by the Division of Christian Education of the National Council of the Churches of Christ in the USA. Used by
permission. All rights reserved.

While any stories in this book are true, some names and identifying information may have been changed to protect the
privacy of individuals.

Cover design: David Fassett
Interior design: Beth McGill

Images: leaf illustration: TongRo/Getty Images
        pastel background: © Gile68/iStockphoto

ISBN 978-0-8308-4131-8 (print)
ISBN 978-0-8308-9341-6 (digital)

Printed in the United States of America ∞

Library of Congress Cataloging-in-Publication Data

Names: Ogden, Greg, author.
Title: Transforming discipleship : making disciples a few at a time / Greg
  Ogden.
Description: Revised and Expanded Edition. | Downers Grove : InterVarsity
  Press, 2016. | Includes bibliographical references.
Identifiers: LCCN 2016011845 (print) | LCCN 2016017716 (ebook) | ISBN
  9780830841318 (pbk. : alk. paper) | ISBN 9780830893416 (eBook)
Subjects: LCSH: Discipling (Christianity)
Classification: LCC BV4520 .O33 2016 (print) | LCC BV4520 (ebook) | DDC
  253—dc23
LC record available at https://lccn.loc.gov/2016011845

P 23 22 21 20 19 18 17 16 15 14 13 12 11 10 9 8 7 6 5 4 3 2 1

Y 36 35 34 33 32 31 30 29 28 27 26 25 24 23 22 21 20 19 18 17 16

To all those I have had the privilege of doing "life together" with in the journey of discipleship in a microgroup over the last thirty years. You have enriched and blessed my life.

CONTENTS

INTRODUCTION

A Story of Transformation

I admit I stumbled onto a discovery, yet it has become one of the most amazing *aha*s of my pastoral ministry. This discovery was the result of an experiment. I had written a first draft of a discipleship curriculum, which turned into the final project for my doctor of ministry degree.[1] The focus of the project was to use this curriculum in the local church and then to evaluate its effectiveness. Up to this point in my ministry I had equated making disciples with a one-to-one relationship. After all, wasn't the Paul–Timothy model the definition of discipling? The point was to grow a disciple who would make a disciple, and so on.

My adviser in the doctoral program suggested that I consider a variety of contexts in which I could test the curriculum and then track the varied dynamics of a discipling relationship. One of the options I chose was to invite two other people to join me on the journey to maturity in Christ. I did not anticipate the potency that would be unleashed in what I have come to call a microgroup (a group of three or four).

It would forever change my understanding of the means the Holy Spirit uses to transform people into Christ's image.

Eric's Story of Transformation

To illustrate the power of microgroups, let me tell the story of Eric's transformation. Eric was one of my first two recruits on this discipleship adventure. He had approached me stating his interest in a mentoring relationship. In retrospect Eric's spiritual ambivalence at the time may not have made him the best candidate for an intensive investment. He was just two years out of college. Looking like a fashion model who had walked straight out of the pages of a men's clothing catalog, Eric was the envy of his male friends. Because of his chiseled good looks, attracting women was either the least of his problems or his greatest temptation, depending how you look at it. He was making more money than he had ever dreamed possible with a promising future with his new company. All of this was quite alluring to him.

Along with the world's enticement, Eric also had a strong pull toward following Christ. It was a matter of who would win this tug of war—Jesus or the world. I mentioned to Eric that I had written a new curriculum and was eager to have some people try it. I made sure he knew that to be involved in this relationship would require an intense investment: a topical study of Scripture and its application to daily life, memorization of Bible verses, and weekly transparent interaction with me and one other person. The bar was set high, yet Eric said he was willing to give it a go.

A restaurant located equidistant between our workplaces became the locale where we were joined by Karl, who at the time was an administrator of an engineering firm. Over lunch we laid our open Bibles and study materials on the restaurant table and proceeded to interact over the content. Immediately, I was impressed by the energetic interchange in our conversation. Something about adding a third party to one-on-one discussions made our conversation come alive. Even though I was the only pastor among the three, I didn't sense that I had to be the focal point or the ever-flowing fountain of wisdom. Our relationship turned into peer discipling in which each of us could honestly share our insights into the Word and its application to our life settings.

Eric was quite open about his divided heart. The enticement of a life of comfort and serial female relationships seemed inviting. He told us about making eye contact with an attractive female motorist while driving through Los Angeles traffic. The next thing he knew, they had pulled off on a side street to exchange phone numbers. Karl and I listened to the story with more than a bit of envy, without any comparable stories to tell. Yet we also understood how seductive sexual power could be for Eric. It was creating a fissure in his heart.

Still, Eric could not get away from the magnetic appeal of Jesus Christ. There was something about the power of the person of Jesus and the life of adventure he has called us to that would not allow Eric to shake him off. In our second lesson we explored Jesus' normative standard for all who would follow him. Jesus said, "If any want to become my followers, let them deny themselves and take up their cross daily and follow me. For those who want to save their life will lose it, and those who lose their life for my sake will save it" (Luke 9:23-24). Eric was faced with the same choice Moses posed to the people of Israel: "See, I have set before you today life and prosperity, death and adversity. . . . Choose life" (Deuteronomy 30:15, 19).

It was not too many weeks into our time together that Eric announced he was going to quit his job and see the world. He wanted to take the better part of a year for a freelance exploration of this planet. In his young, carefree and unattached years he desired to do what he might not be able to do later when more responsibilities would weigh on him. He reasoned that he could always get a job when he returned, but this stage of his life would come only once. This decision precipitated some forthright interchange. It was evident that Eric was drifting into a life of self-absorption. Searching for a way to speak to his wanderlust, I said, "Eric, at least consider taking a month or two of this time to invest somewhere in a mission opportunity. Pause long enough to immerse yourself in God's work in your travels and rub shoulders with some amazing servants of Christ who are giving themselves away for the sake of the gospel."

I don't remember the exact sequence of events or steps in the shift, but before I knew it, Eric decided to abandon his vagabond plans. The shift of focus was startling and dramatic. He signed on for a summer mission opportunity with Campus Crusade for Christ (now CRU) in Hungary and Poland. This was prior to the fall of communism in Eastern Europe. I have often reflected on the power of being able to speak a word of truth or challenge into a life. If we had not had the regularity of relationship and the trust that had been built in those few months, I doubt that Eric would have had a context in which to hear a confrontative word that had the potential to redirect his life.

When Eric returned that summer from his adventures, he was transformed. His divided heart had become singularly subsumed under the
lordship of Jesus. Eric regaled us with stories of sharing the gospel on
the lakeside beaches of Hungary and stealthy forays into Poland. People
were hungry for the good news, and he saw Jesus Christ grab hold of
and redirect lives, not the least of which was his own.

Upon his return Eric immediately joined the Campus Crusade staff
with the intent of taking business people into the Eastern-bloc countries
in order to crack open their hearts to the work of the life-changing
gospel in these barricaded regions. At the same time he reconnected
with a high school sweetheart, who also was a passionate follower of
Jesus. It seemed only a matter of months before they were engaged and
Betsy was ready to join Eric on staff with Campus Crusade. These two
lit up rooms with their radiant joy in service to Christ and their love for
each other. They honored me by asking me to perform their wedding in
Portland, Oregon, alongside Betsy's pastor.

A number of weeks prior to the wedding, Eric was experiencing de-
bilitating back pain, which he assumed was caused by a recent motor-
cycle accident. Even with physical therapy, however, he was showing no
improvement. On the Monday prior to their Saturday wedding, the
source of the back pain was discovered. A tumor was pressing against
Eric's spine. Testicular cancer had spread to multiple parts of his body.
The prognosis was not good. He was admitted to the hospital that same
day and began a heavy regimen of chemotherapy.

Of course, Eric and Betsy had some immediate decisions to make.
Would the wedding proceed? Yes, Eric and Betsy's spirits were undaunted. Where should the wedding be held? This called for a quick
change of venue. The church wedding was replaced by the hospital
chapel, which could hold a standing-room-only crowd. The scene could
have been something out of a made-for-TV movie designed to manip-
ulate emotions. But this was real life. Eric's hospital bed was rolled into
the chapel with Eric propped up at an almost ninety-degree angle. The
bed covers came up to his waist, with his upper torso appropriately
dressed in his tuxedo. Betsy, his bride, stood bedside, holding Eric's hand
in her right hand and her bouquet in the left. The wedding party flanked

the bed on either side. There is usually considerable anticipation at weddings, but rarely is the air as thick with lump-in-the-throat emotions as it was in this packed chapel. Now three decades after this event, I have no trouble remembering the thickness in my windpipe and the struggle to focus on my notes through my misty eyes.

In the ensuing months the chemotherapy took a toll on this handsome man. On his better days Eric was able to travel. I still have vivid images of him walking into our Southern California church with his knit cap covering his billiard-ball head, and looking gaunt. Yet his spirit was undaunted. He radiated the indwelling presence of Jesus Christ. I knew that this was a man living the words of the apostle Paul, "So we do not lose heart. Even though our outer nature is wasting away, our inner nature is being renewed day by day" (2 Corinthians 4:16).

When things took a turn for the worse and Eric had to go back into the hospital for further treatments, I flew to Portland to visit him. As I was walking toward Eric's hospital room, some of his buddies from high school were exiting. These young men, who could normally make light of anything, were unusually sullen. One of them said to me, "You know what Eric said? He said this cancer is the best thing that ever happened to him. Can you believe that?" Eric obviously would have preferred it otherwise, but he had come to cast his entire hope upon Jesus Christ, and his Lord and Lover had not let him down.

In a note to me, Eric said of his discoveries,

God is helping me grow closer to him. It [the cancer] has made me realize whom I have to depend on. And I have seen through these experiences that when I do call upon God that he really helps in his way. It may not mean that he will relieve the pain or that he will cure the cancer immediately. It may mean that I die, or live . . . that does not matter. What is important is that I keep my eyes on him.

One morning a doctor came in when Betsy was with me and said, "I want to tell you the X-rays are not very encouraging. You may want to consider getting things in order and stopping treatment." This was the first time it occurred to me that I might die. I might not live through this.

It really caused me to reassess what I am placing my faith in. Am I placing my faith in the doctors and drugs, or am I placing my faith in God? If I am placing my faith in God, I have the assurance that he will deliver me out of the situation I am in. . . . It may not mean that he will cure the cancer or that I will survive. . . . But that is not what is important. It goes back to keeping my eyes on him.

On April 25, 1986, seven months after his marriage to Betsy, Eric died at the age of twenty-five. Here was a man who in a short time went from ambivalence about following Jesus Christ to wholehearted trust and devotion.

Our Journey of Transformation

I introduce this book with Eric's story because in essence the change in Eric is what this book is about—the process and context for transformation into Christlikeness. What I stumbled into with Eric and Karl opened up for me an exploratory journey into the optimum settings and ingredients necessary to create the conditions for being conformed to the image of Christ. Since this initial experience I have witnessed repeatedly the power of microgroups. They provide the setting to bring together the necessary elements for transformation or growth to maturity in Christ. What have I observed in this setting?

- Multiplication or reproduction: empowering those who are discipled to disciple others

- Intimate relationships: developing deep trust as the soil for life change

- Accountability: lovingly speaking truth into another's life

- Incorporation of the biblical message: covering the themes of Scripture sequentially to create a holistic picture of the Christian life

- Spiritual disciplines: practicing the habits that lead to intimacy with Christ and service to others

This book will introduce to you a missing tool in the arsenal of disciple making that will lead to life-transforming experiences such as Eric's. For three decades I have had at least one microgroup as a part of my weekly schedule. Never do I feel more fulfilled as a pastor than when I am sharing my life with two or three others who are on an intentional journey to maturity in Christ. Seeing these same partners empowered to disciple others so that multiple generations of Christians are firmly rooted and reproduce is about as good as it gets!

I am excited about the discoveries that lie ahead for you. In the ensuing pages you will learn a simple, reproducible approach to making disciples. This approach is grounded in the biblical model of Jesus and Paul, who intentionally grew followers into responsible, reproducing disciples and disciple makers.

In chapters one and two we will examine the urgency of this issue. Bill Hull has prophetically written, "The crisis at the heart of the church is a crisis of product."[2] *Disciple making, discipleship* and *discipling* are hot topics today, because we see such a great need for this focus in our churches. A sign of the felt need for intentional disciple making was the response that occurred the first time I co-taught a course titled "Growing a Disciple-Making Congregation." Usually it takes some time for new classes to catch on, because students don't want to be lab rats in new course development. Students usually wait to hear from others how it went. Not so with this class. We had one of our largest classes during my tenure as director of this program. Why? There is an evident discipleship deficit in our churches and ministries that we know needs to be addressed, but we are not sure how to do so.

Chapter one examines the symptoms of the discipleship deficit, while chapter two will attempt to unearth the root causes of these symptoms. The intent of this rather sobering discussion is not to air the church's dirty laundry or condemn Christian leaders. Who needs more self-flagellation? Yet the first step toward recovering Jesus' mission statement for the church, "Go and make disciples," is to evaluate the scope of the need. A sober assessment of the gap between Jesus' stated end and our practice will define the cost for completing the task. The first two chapters provide tools for you to assess the symptoms and causes of the discipleship deficit in your church or ministry.

In chapters three through five we will explore Jesus' and Paul's approaches to making disciples as a guide for our disciple making. In spite of highly readable and insightful works on Jesus' and Paul's strategies of growing followers, Christian leaders do not seem to translate this into workable ministry practice.[3] In all of my teaching through seminars and courses on making disciples Jesus' way, I still sense that a small percentage of pastors and church leaders emulate Jesus' and Paul's models. So it is worth asking again, how did transformation take place in those who traveled with Jesus and Paul on their itinerant ministries? Jesus staked the future of his ministry on his investment in a few. Do we do the same? Why did Jesus choose the Twelve and spend so much time with them? If we were to follow this model, what would it look like? Today, we can name those who were trainees and partners in Paul's ministry. What does this say about the way we should carry out our ministry? When we can make evident connections between the scriptural models and our ministry practice, the people of God get the picture in a powerful way.

Once the biblical model of Jesus and Paul has refreshed our theological vision, we will see how the imperative to make disciples a few at a time can be become integral to our church- or ministry-based approach. Chapters six through eight will examine three of the critical issues that need to be addressed in any disciple-making strategy. First, disciple making is about *relational investment*. It is walking alongside a few fellow travelers in an intentional journey together over time. You will hear this constant refrain: *Disciple making is not a program but a relationship.*

Second, we rightly associate disciple making with *multiplication*. Yet the promise always seems to far exceed the results. Discipleship programs are sold to us with the promise that disciples will be multiplied through intergenerational transference from life to life. The reality is that we rarely get beyond the first generation. Yet we have not made disciples if we only help people grow to maturity without also seeing them reproduce. I have lived the frustration of not seeing those I have invested in go on to disciple others. I have also witnessed some wonderful breakthroughs of empowerment. I am eager to share these discoveries with you.

Third, making disciples is a *transformative process*. I will identify the convergence of the key ingredients that make transformation of a life by the Holy Spirit possible, as in Eric's case. What ingredients placed Eric's life in the transformative laboratory of the Holy Spirit? When we bring together *transparent relationships* and *the truth of God's Word* in the context of *covenantal accountability* for life change around a *missional focus*, we have stepped into the Holy Spirit's hot house that makes life change possible.

The three elements of relational investment, multiplication and a transformative process come together powerfully in the model of reproducible microgroups.

In chapter nine we look at the steps necessary for a church- or ministry-based discipling strategy. The following practical questions are addressed: What is a workable disciple-making model? Whom should we invite into the discipling process? How do we get started? How can we grow a multigenerational network of disciples? How do we keep up the motivation for multiplication through the generations?

Finally, in chapter ten we will explore the critical contributions and limitations of preaching in the disciple-making process.

Some of you don't need to be convinced that there is a disciple deficit in your churches; neither do you need to revisit the biblical vision for how disciples are made. You are looking for a practical strategy to make it happen. I will not be offended if you leap over the first two parts of the book and go directly to the last section, which is designed to assist you in practical implementation of a disciple-making strategy.

Since first stumbling on the power of microgroups with Eric and Karl almost three decades ago, I have had the privilege to walk with many others in this life-altering relationship and observe the growth of multigenerational discipling networks in three churches. Over this period I have heard from people across North America and around the world whose lives and ministries have been radically changed because they employed multiplying microgroups. In spite of the enormous discipleship challenge facing the church, I am encouraged by the considerable desire to make disciples. When the urgency for disciple making can be fanned by the vision of the biblical pattern of investing in a few at a time and then translated into a practical strategy, there is the hope that we can truly fulfill Jesus' mission statement for everyone in his church, "Go therefore and make disciples of all nations" (Matthew 28:19).

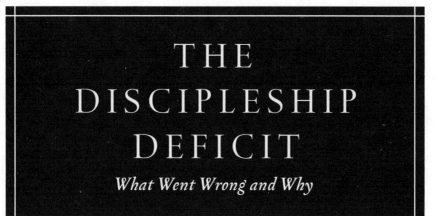

PART ONE

THE DISCIPLESHIP DEFICIT

What Went Wrong and Why

1

THE DISCIPLESHIP GAP

Where Have All the Disciples Gone?

I was intrigued by the cover story of the June 2013 edition of *Christianity Today*, which asked "Does Child Sponsorship Work?"[1] Since my wife and I have sponsored children for forty years and are currently engaged with three different organizations, I had a vested interest in the answer. The author of this article, Bruce Wydick, professor of economics and international studies at the University of San Francisco, was responding to a question he would often get: "What can the ordinary person do to help the poor?" He reflexive response was, "Sponsor a child." Then he realized that as an economist he had never scientifically tested whether sponsored children were any better off in the long run than unsponsored children. This prompted him to search for a graduate student who would take this on as a PhD project. He found the student, but was surprised with how difficult it was to do the research. When Wydick's PhD student approached several relief organizations, only one agreed to be evaluated. Even this lone organization would only do so under the condition of anonymity. I frankly was more than miffed when I read this article. I wanted to call up one relief organization I had been with for almost forty years and give them a piece of my mind. What do you mean you don't want to know whether your organization is actually making a difference?

But then it dawned on me that it requires courage to face the truth about myself or even the churches I have served. Have you ever asked someone for honest feedback, and he or she says to you, "Well, do you want the truth or would you rather I make you feel good?" Everything in me screams, "Lie and make me feel good!" But once I have settled down, I sheepishly say, "Okay, break it to me gently."

Bill Hybels, founding pastor of Willow Creek Community Church, often says, "Facts are your friends." Willow Creek Church lives up to this motto. Among the many things I admire about them is their desire to live in reality, no matter how painful that may be. In 2004 they did an internal audit, which later became the REVEAL Spiritual Life Survey.[2] It revealed some glaring gaps in their self-image. Ministries and programs they thought were effective were, in fact, ineffective.[3] But they had the mettle to allow the truth to provide course corrections.

The State of Discipleship Today: You Are Here!

This chapter is designed to help you do the sober work of finding out where you are. Unless we can see the gap between current reality and our desired destination, we won't be able to assess what it will take to get there. Business leader Max DePree says, "The first responsibility of a leader is to define reality."[4] Jesus himself commended this approach, saying, "Suppose one of you wants to build a tower. Won't you first sit down and estimate the cost to see if you have enough money to complete it?" (Luke 14:28 NIV). When I was directing a Doctor of Ministry Program, the counsel I would give students at the final project phase was to spend a considerable amount of time defining the need, challenge or problem they were trying to address. I told them to write, rewrite and write again a one-paragraph summary of their focus until the need they were addressing was crystal clear. Similarly, only as we get the need internalized will we be motivated to marshal the necessary resources to complete the disciple-making call.

Most of us have had the experience of searching for a particular store in a shopping mall. In order to find our desired location, we first look for the mall directory. Once the store is pinpointed on the map, we need to identify where we are in order to plot our course. Usually a red dot marks our location with an arrow and the words "You Are Here." Only when we know where we are can we see where we are going.

My own one-word summary of our current state of discipleship is *superficial.* Tim Stafford, senior writer for *Christianity Today*, asked the late John Stott how he would evaluate the enormous growth of the church since he had been ordained sixty-one years earlier. Stott replied, "The answer is 'growth without depth.' None of us wants to dispute the extraordinary growth of the church. But it has been largely numerical and statistical growth. And there has not been sufficient growth in discipleship that is comparable to the growth in numbers."[5] Having taught internationally in Asia, Central America and Europe, the repeated lament I hear is that we are much better at conversion than we are at transformation of these converts into disciples of Jesus.

This *superficiality* comes into focus when we observe the incongruity between the numbers of people in America who profess faith in Jesus Christ and the lack of impact on the moral and spiritual climate of our times. The Pew Research Center's 2015 study notes that still 70.6 percent of American population identifies themselves as Christian, with 25.4 percent categorized as evangelical.[6] The Pew study classifies someone as evangelical if they are member of Pew's defined list of evangelical denominations or that have identified themselves as "born again" or "evangelical" in their interviews. The Barna Group, an overtly Christian polling organization, comes at these statistics somewhat differently. They make a distinction between "born again" and "evangelical."[7] The Barna Group has shown a fairly consistent figure of four out of ten adult Americans who would say they are "born again." For Barna a person is "born again" if their personal commitment to Christ is currently significant and they believe they will go to heaven based on confession of their sin and trusting in Christ for salvation. And yet with this significant percentage of professed Christ-followers, there is a lot of handwringing among Christian leaders about the spiritual state of American culture. I am suggesting that the lack of Christian influence on culture is a direct result of the lack of depth of transformative discipleship.

Barna has sadly concluded, "My research shows that most Americans who confess their sins to God and ask Christ to be their Savior—live almost indistinguishable from the unrepentant sinners, and their lives bear little, if any fruit, for the kingdom of God."[8]

To repeat Bill Hull's prophetic word, "The crisis at the heart of the church today is a crisis of product."[9] What kind of followers of Jesus are we producing? How deep is our discipleship deficit?

Before we even consider proposing a solution, we need to do the hard work of self-examination. Before we can get a handle on our ministry, we need to check the directory for the arrow that says, "You Are Here." To help you do this, I have chosen seven biblical marks of discipleship as the grid for this self-evaluation.[10] With each of these qualities I will sketch the biblical ideal and then examine some indicators of reality we might see within our ministry communities. At the end of each section you have the opportunity to look at your ministry setting through the lens of each of the biblical marks and give yourself a grade on the quality of discipleship you witness among the people you serve. The biblical marks of discipleship are

- Ministers: Passive vs. Proactive
- Christian Life: Casual vs. Disciplined
- Discipleship: Private vs. Holistic
- Culture: Conformed vs. Transformed
- Church: Optional vs. Essential
- Bible: Illiterate vs. Informed
- Witness: Inactive vs. Active

Ministers: Passive versus proactive. The Scripture portrays the church as full of proactive ministers; the reality often is that majority of church members see themselves as passive recipients of the pastor's ministry.

The New Testament pictures the church as an every-member ministry. The "priesthood of all believers" is not just a Reformation watchword but a biblical ideal. Writing to scattered, persecuted Christians, Peter refers to the church in aggregate when he writes, "You [plural] are . . . a royal priesthood" (1 Peter 2:9). Every believer comes to God via Christ, their Mediator (vertical dimension), and every believer is enabled to act as a priest on behalf of fellow members of the body of Christ (horizontal dimension). Ministry that is biblically envisioned calls up images not of the paid priests (pastors) hugging ministry to themselves, but views ministry in the hands of ordinary saints. The apostle Paul has the everyday Christian in mind when he writes, "To each is given the manifestation of the Spirit for the common good" (1 Corinthians 12:7). Playing off the image of the church as the body of Christ, Paul says that the Holy Spirit has given all believers ministry gifts, and therefore each believer is equivalent to a body part that contributes to the health of the whole. The New Testament describes a full employment plan that dignifies and gives all believers value based on the contribution their gifts make in building up and extending the church.

The reality is that the 80-20 rule applies to many of our congregations.[11] Churches fight against the barrier where 20 percent of the people provide ministry for the 80 percent who are recipients, and 20 percent who give 80 percent of the finances. In *The Other 80 Percent*, Scott Thumma and Warren Bird observe that the 80 percent who evidence limited engagement fall into three categories: (1) 10-20 percent of the congregation are declining in participation (often have left a role and no longer feel needed); (2) fully one-third have low or marginal participation levels (these are occasional attenders); (3) the remaining percentage are infrequent attenders who are the long-term prodigal members, often struggling with a particular need that is unknown to the leadership. This is confirmed by the fact that most denominations combined worship attendance averages between 20 and 50 percent of their official membership. Yet the good news from this research shows that when asked, many of 80 percent long to be involved, trained, given responsibility and inspired to Christian service. Churches often do not have the methods in place to engage these who could be drawn in. The church today has been compared to a football game with twenty-two people on the field in desperate need of rest, and fifty thousand people in the stands in desperate need of exercise.

This 80-20 pattern is reinforced by the spectator mentality we have fostered in our "main event," corporate worship. As a pastor I am consciously aware that people arrive at worship with a reviewer's mentality. Worshipers believe it's the responsibility of those on stage to provide an engaging, meaningful and entertaining show, while the worshipers' role is to give an instant review of the worship service as they pass through the receiving line after worship. We are so used to this pattern that it doesn't seem odd for people to make evaluative comments like "Good sermon, Pastor" or "I enjoyed the service today." My favorite evaluation

I received was, "You know, you're getting better!" (It wasn't my favorite at the time.) What does this tell us about the dynamic that has been created? It's a spectator-performer arrangement.

The apostle Paul describes a full-employment plan within the body of Christ. Every member of the body comes to know his or her value through the exercise of spiritual gifts. To the extent that members of the body are not playing their part, the whole body suffers. In congregational surveys the good news is that 68 percent of born-again Christians have heard of spiritual gifts; this is raised to 99 percent for evangelicals, according to Barna. Yet the level of engagement among those who are born again is not encouraging. A full 20 percent of respondents named gifts that had little biblical correlation: sense of humor, singing, patience, a job and so on. "Between those who do not know their gift (15%), those who say they don't have one (28%) and those who claimed gifts that are not biblical (20%), nearly two-thirds of the self-identified Christian population who claim to have heard about spiritual gifts have not been able to accurately apply whatever they have heard or what the Bible teaches on the subject to their lives."[12] This would indicate a significant percentage of "unemployed" believers in our ministries.

When you examine your own ministry, what percentage of people do you think could name their spiritual gifts and are exercising them in a context of ministry? Does the 80-20 rule describe your reality, or are you experiencing a breakthrough beyond this limit? Please respond by using figure 1.1.

Rate your ministry on a scale of 1 to 5, 1 being passive recipients and 5 being proactive ministers.		
Discipleship Symptom	**Rating**	**Notes**
Ministers: Passive vs. Proactive		

Figure 1.1. Passive versus proactive

Christian Life: Casual versus disciplined. The Scriptures picture followers of Jesus as engaged in a disciplined way of life; the reality is that a small percentage of believers invests in intentional spiritual growth practices.

Great and accomplished athletes perform effortlessly. Having lived for ten years in Chicago, I repeatedly heard stories from Chicagoland residents about the best basketball player ever to grace the hardwood, Michael Jordan. Even though Michael Jordan was endowed by God with remarkable athletic prowess, he did not rely on it. What people did not see was his work ethic. He had the reputation of being the first one in the gym and the last one out.

In the New Testament the discipline of an athlete is one of the consistent images for the Christian life. Comparing the Christian life with a race, Paul writes, "Do you not know that in a race all the runners run, but only one gets the prize? Everyone who competes in the games goes into strict training. They do it to get a crown that will not last, we do it to get a crown that will last forever" (1 Corinthians 9:24-25 NIV). Note Paul's "how much more" argument for how we are to approach our life in Christ. If athletes put themselves through a rigorous regimen to get a "crown that will not last," *how much more* should Christians discipline ourselves, because our goal is "a crown that will last forever." The writer to the Hebrews urges believers to move beyond being milk-drinking infants to adult believers who can take in solid food. Using a similar image of the gymnasium and athletic exertion, the author of Hebrews writes, "But solid food is for the mature, for those whose faculties have been trained by practice to distinguish good from evil" (Hebrews 5:14).

Dallas Willard captures this attitude toward training with a pithy phrase: "Grace is opposed to earning, but is not opposed to effort."[13] This is why the practices employed to develop our discipleship are called *spiritual disciplines.*

It is common within the evangelical world to urge the practice of personal spiritual disciplines. In the most recent survey on "the state of discipleship" only 20 percent of all Christian adults were in involved in one of the following four discipleship activities: (1) Sunday school or fellowship group (43%); (2) spiritual mentor (17%); (3) study the Bible in a group (33%); and (4) reading or discussing a Christian book (25%).[14] In a recent survey only 19 percent of self-identified Christians made daily Scripture reading a habit.[15] Disciplines can also take the form of relational engagements such as a mentoring relationship, a small group or more stringent intentional discipleship groups. Yet only 21 percent of self-identified Christians believe that "spiritual maturity requires a vital connection to a community of faith."[16] Of those who stated that spiritual growth was important to them, 37 percent said they preferred to do it on their own and that their spiritual growth was "entirely private," meaning they kept it to themselves.[17]

Discipline implies intention and a plan of action. According to Barna, fewer than one in five born-again adults have any specific, measurable goals related to their spiritual development. In Barna's nationwide survey, interviews were conducted with hundreds of people, including pastors and church leaders, who regularly attended church services and programs. Barna concludes, "Not one of the adults we interviewed said that their goal in life was to be a committed follower of Jesus Christ or to make disciples of the entire world—or even their entire block."[18] When this group was asked what they wanted to accomplish in life, eight out of ten believers found success in family, career development and financial achievement. This is hardly distinguishable from the American dream. Dallas Willard observes, "The fact is that there is now lacking a serious and expectant intention to bring Jesus' people into obedience and abundance through training."[19]

As you observe your congregation, where would you place your people on the casual-versus-disciplined spectrum? Please respond by using figure 1.2.

Rate your ministry on a scale of 1 to 5, with 1 being spiritually casual and 5 being spiritually disciplined.		
Discipleship Symptom	**Rating**	**Notes**
Christian Life: Casual vs. Disciplined		

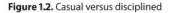

Figure 1.2. Casual versus disciplined

Discipleship: Private versus holistic. The Scriptures picture discipleship as affecting all spheres of life; the reality is that many believers have relegated faith to the personal, private realm.

The dominant theme of Jesus' public ministry was the proclamation of the good news of the kingdom of God. The future, long-awaited kingdom, where the rule and reign of God will be actualized on earth, had broken into the present darkness in the person of the King, Jesus Christ. The promise is that those who "repent and believe" the gospel (Mark 1:15) are transferred from the kingdom of darkness to the kingdom of the beloved Son (Colossians 1:13). A new authority is established in the hearts of Jesus' followers. The motif of the kingdom is that there is not a scintilla of life that does not come under the authority of Jesus Christ. Fundamentally, we are kingdom people, which means that Jesus is Lord in our hearts, homes and workplaces; our attitudes, thoughts and desires; our relationships and moral decisions; our political convictions and social conscience. In every area of our interior life, personal relationships or social involvement, we seek to know and live the mind and will of God.

Yet the reality is that we suffer today from the same bifurcated existence that Martin Luther addressed five hundred years ago with Reformation force. In writing his *Open Letter to the German Nobility*, Luther said that the first barrier erected by the Roman Catholic Church was a false distinction between what he called the "spiritual estate" and "temporal estate."[20] In Luther's day the spiritual estate was the realm of the Church and its holy orders, which took precedence over and elevated itself above the temporal estate, which was the realm of government and the common life. Luther attempted to break down the wall between the sacred and secular, declaring that in kingdom terms everything is sacred. The dividing line is not between sacred and secular but between the kingdom of God and the kingdom of darkness.

Yet it appears that we still suffer under the false notion that the religious or sacred realm is relegated to a private sphere, which consists of church, family and the interior life. When a believer moves into the social, secular realm, it is as if an entirely different set of assumptions are adopted. Personal faith is often minimized in the workplace, in determining our political convictions and in the way we view other social institutions that govern public life (for example, economics, education and media). Os Guinness summarizes this disconnect between personal faith and the totality of life by saying that our faith is "privately engaging but socially irrelevant."[21]

There is a disconnect between our faith and the workplace. Few people understand the faith-workplace dynamic the way one of my friends does: "I am a disciple of Jesus masquerading as a furniture salesman." Sure his job is to sell furniture, but his calling is to follow Jesus in all that he does. William Diehl, formerly an executive with Bethlehem Steel and a strong proponent of Christian witness and service in the workplace, writes these words of frustration that unfortunately are all too common,

> In almost thirty years of my professional career, my church has never once suggested that there be any type of accounting of my on-the-job ministry to others. My church has never once offered to improve those skills, which could make me a better minister, nor has it ever asked if I need any kind of support in what I am doing. There never has been an enquiry into the types of ethical decisions I must face, or whether I seek to communicate faith to my co-workers. I have never been in a congregation where there was any type of public affirmation of my ministry in my career. In short, I must conclude that my church doesn't have the least interest whether or how I minister in my daily work.[22]

How would you assess the view of discipleship among those you rub elbows with? Is faith relegated to a private, interior realm, or do you sense that faith in Christ is allowed to seep into all aspects of life? Please respond by using figure 1.3.

Rate your view of discipleship on a scale of 1 to 5, 1 being private (limited to personal realms) and 5 being holistic (encompassing all of life).		
Discipleship Symptom	**Rating**	**Notes**
Discipleship: Private vs. Holistic		

Figure 1.3. Private versus holistic

Church: Conformed versus transformed. The Scriptures picture the Christian community as a countercultural force; the reality is that we see isolated individuals whose lifestyle and values are not much different from those of the unchurched.

John Stott has described the church of the Lord's intention as a community of "radical nonconformity" or a "contrast society." These phrases are a helpful summary of some of the biblical metaphors for the church. The images of "alien," "exile" and "sojourner" capture the relationship of believers to this present world (1 Peter 2:11). This sentiment is expressed in the words of the old hymn "This world is not my home, I'm just a-passing through."[23] The church in the biblical scheme is a body whose collective lifestyle forms a countercultural alternative to the values of the dominant society.

The apostle Peter gave us a word picture for this new reality when he addressed the church dispersed across the landscape of the Greco-Roman world. Though these believers in Jesus did not have a land to call their own, he could still say to them, "You are . . . a holy nation" (1 Peter 2:9). By using this image Peter was saying, "You are a people who cut across all geopolitical boundaries, because you are a church without borders." To be holy is to be a called-out people, meaning separate or different. One of the distinguishing features of this new kingdom people is their lifestyle of compassionate and costly service. Echoing Jesus' words in the Sermon on the Mount (Matthew 5:16), Peter says, "Conduct yourselves honorably among the Gentiles, so that, though they malign you as evildoers, they may see your honorable deeds and glorify God when he comes to judge" (1 Peter 2:12). Those hostile to the church may not affirm what we believe, but they can't argue against the way we live.

If this was true then, what might people observe about the church in our day? Too often when it comes to moral values or lifestyle choices the churched and the unchurched appear almost indistinguishable. Ron Sider introduces his book *The Scandal of the Evangelical Conscience* with this devastating summary: "Whether the issue is divorce, materialism, sexual promiscuity, racism, physical abuse in marriage, or neglect of biblical worldview, the polling data point to widespread, blatant disobedience of clear biblical moral demands on the part of people who allegedly are evangelical, born-again Christians."[24] It would appear that Christians have been almost as seduced by self-focus as the broader population. Eighty-four percent of adults and 66 percent of Christians agreed that "the highest goal in life is to enjoy it as much as possible." In addition, 91 percent of adults and 76 percent of Christians believe that "the best way to find yourself is to look inside yourself." David Kinnaman concludes that "if we peel back the layers, many Christians are using the Way of Jesus as a means to pursuing the Way of Self."[25]

If the church is intended to be a "contrast society," then it needs to shape and instill the values of the kingdom in the set-apart people. This requires a church culture with a clear disciple-making agenda supported by a covenantal mentality. Yet increasingly this reality has been undermined by radical individualism. Being a part of a covenantal community is countered by the American ideal of independence. Each person keeps his or her own counsel and determines his or her own beliefs. Eighty-one percent of the American people said they are able to arrive at their own religious views without regard to a body of believers.[26] The idea of being accountable to a group of Christ-followers—to whom we give permission to keep us faithful to our commitments and disciplines—seems all too rare. How can we possibly build countercultural communities out of such porous material?

How would you assess the lifestyles of the believers in your network of relationships? Does it appear that there is little difference in values and priorities from the dominant society, or do you see your fellow believers as lights shining in the darkness? Please respond by using figure 1.4.

Rate your church community on a scale of 1 to 5, 1 conformed to this world and 5 being transformed into contrast society.		
Discipleship Symptom	Rating	Notes
Church: Conformed vs. Transformed		

Figure 1.4. Conformed versus transformed

Church: Optional versus essential. The Scriptures picture the church as an essential, chosen organism in whom Christ dwells; the reality is that people view the church as an optional institution, unnecessary for discipleship.

The church of Jesus Christ is nothing less than his corporate replacement on earth. Jesus continues his incarnation by dwelling in his people. The late Ray Stedman succinctly described Christ's relationship to the church: "The life of Jesus is still being manifest among people, but now no longer through an individual physical body, limited to one place on earth, but through a complex, corporate body called the church."[27] The apostle Paul's favorite and most fundamental image for the church is that of the body of Christ. When Paul uses this term, it is far more than a nice word picture or metaphor. He is not saying that the church is *like* the body of Christ but that it literally *is* the body of Christ. This is the place where Christ continues to dwell.

The implication is that the church is not an optional afterthought for those who name Christ as their Lord. The church is central to God's plan of salvation. God saves people into a new community, which is the vanguard of a new humanity. To be called to Christ is to throw one's lot in with his people. Many people today like to say, "Jesus, yes; church, no." To do so is a fundamental misunderstanding of the place the church has in God's grand scheme of salvation. To be a follower of Christ is to understand that there is no such thing as solo discipleship.

Yet it appears that in our communication of the gospel we have separated following Christ from the necessity of being integrally involved in a church community. David Platt describes an evangelistic event where the preacher was driving to a conclusion, crafting his call to decision. "Tonight, I want to call you to put your faith in God. I am urging you to begin a personal relationship with Jesus. But let me be clear. I'm not inviting you to join the church. I'm inviting you to come to Christ."[28] Implicit in this invitation was that you might be able to carry on a relationship with Christ apart from the church. Apparently this preacher's perspective is shared by a significant number of Christians as well. In response to the statement "You cannot become a complete and mature person unless you belong to a community of faith that influences you," only 18 percent strongly agreed with this statement.[29]

We are a nation of church shoppers. Joshua Harris says that we have adopted a "dating the church" mentality. Dating means we keep our options open. Though we are in this relationship now, we keep scouring the horizon to see if something better may come along. We don't want to close off our options and make a covenantal commitment. Our current relationship with a church is based on whether it meets our needs or checks the boxes of what we are looking for in a church. The implication is if things change, then we can make a change as well. Christian leaders live with the tension of serving a community of people with a tenuous commitment. How can you call people to the discipline of discipleship if they can so easily walk? Juan Carlos Ortiz observes that we could not be effective parents if our children could decide they were going to become a part of another family if they didn't like the discipline in the home.[30] Unless a commitment to a church community is similar to the covenant of marriage, how can people be formed into Christlike disciples?

How would you assess people's understanding of the church in God's grand scheme? Is the church simply a helpful option, or is it viewed as central to God's plan of salvation? Please respond by using figure 1.5.

Rate the commitment to the church as a covenant community on a scale of 1 to 5, 1 being optional and 5 being essential.		
Discipleship Symptom	**Rating**	**Notes**
Church: Optional vs. Essential		

Figure 1.5. Optional versus essential

Bible: Illiterate versus informed. Followers of Christ are often called "the people of the book" because we believe the Scriptures of the Old and New Testament to be the unique written revelation of God; the reality is that believers' knowledge of Scripture is woefully inadequate.

The Bible is the trustworthy depository of God's self-revelation to humanity. We look to Scripture as "the only infallible rule of faith and practice." In other words, if we want to know God's mind on how to live, this is what we base our life on. Scripture is the record of God's unfolding story in history, the witness to the nature of his character, and how we obtain that which is "able to make [us] wise for salvation through faith in Christ Jesus" (2 Timothy 3:15 NIV). We look to Scripture to give us the most reliable answers to these worldview questions: (1) How did our world come to be? (2) Why are we here? (3) What went wrong? (4) How can it be made right? (5) Where is it all going? We preach the Scripture from the pulpit, make it the center of our small group discoveries and include it as part of our daily spiritual diet because the Bible is to the soul what food is to our bodies.

Americans have a high view of Scripture. Almost 50 percent believe that Scripture contains everything a person needs to lead a meaningful life. Almost 60 percent believe that the Bible has had the most impact on history. From a list of words to describe the Bible, the word *inspired* far exceeds any other option. When Americans are asked to name a sacred text, 79 percent say the Bible, which is eight times more than any other sacred text, such as the Koran.[31]

Yet with all these lofty claims, the Bible is far more revered than it is read. Only 14 percent read the Bible on a daily basis, and another 14 percent several times a week. Just 12 percent consider themselves highly knowledgeable of the Bible. The reality of people's biblical knowledge is far different from what we say we believe about it. Kenneth Berding, New Testament professor at Talbot School of Theology, says,

> All the research indicates that biblical literacy in America is at an all-time low. My own experience of teaching a class of new college freshmen every year for the past fifteen years suggests to me that although students fifteen years ago knew little about the Bible upon entering my classes, today's students on average know even less about the Bible.[32]

Only 43 percent from the "State of the Bible 2015" study could name the first five books of the Bible, and about the same percentage thought that John the Baptist was one of the apostles. Only about 25 percent could recognize Jesus' affirmation "the truth shall set you free" as a quote from Scripture. Sometimes this misinformation can be somewhat humorous. Berding recalls a student who did not realize that King Saul of the Old Testament was different from Saul, later Paul, in the New Testament. Another student referenced Joshua, the son of a nun, not aware that "Nun" referred to Joshua's father, not a Roman Catholic community of women.

The concern this raises, as Berding highlights, is that there is a famine of God's Word even in the church; we are starving ourselves to death. Instead of following the admonition to meditate on God's law day and night (Joshua 1:8; Psalm 1:2; 119:97), we take a haphazard approach to internalizing the Word in our lives. Through prophet Amos the Lord warns,

"The days are coming," declares the Sovereign LORD,
  "when I will send a famine through the land—
not a famine of food or a thirst for water,
  but a famine of hearing the words of the LORD." (Amos 8:11 NIV)

In Amos's era God was going to withhold the word, but in our time we have unlimited access and yet are starving ourselves to death.

How would you assess the place of Scripture in the daily diet of the fellow believers you know? Please respond by using figure 1.6.

Rate your ministry on the extent of the knowledge of God's Word on a scale of 1 to 5, 1 being illiterate and 5 informed.		
Discipleship Symptom	**Rating**	**Notes**
Bible: Illiterate vs. Informed		

Figure 1.6. Illiterate versus informed

Witness: Inactive versus active. The Scriptures picture all believers as those who share the story of their faith in Christ with others; the reality is that a relatively small percentage of believers make it their intention to do so.

We are storytellers. The Bible spins a love story of God's pursuit of wayward humanity. Those of us captured by Jesus Christ have a story to tell of how God chased us down and embraced us in his loving arms. In so doing, the Lord has included us as characters in his grand redemptive drama. We each have an assigned part to play on the stage of history, which is the realm in which God writes his story. This story makes sense of why we are here. As unique as each of us is, there is a common story line written into the script for each of our lives. "You will be my witnesses," Jesus says (Acts 1:8). We each have our story and *the* story to tell, for as we share our story and *the* story, others find that they too have been written into this redemptive drama. Paul could not be clearer about the privilege we have when he wrote that the gospel "is the power of God for salvation" (Romans 1:16). God has entrusted us with the story of the visited planet, and telling it is the means he uses to melt human hearts.

How are we doing in telling the story? The picture here is somewhat unclear. When born again Christians are asked if they have a personal responsibility to share their faith in Christ, 73 percent say they do. Fifty-two percent of born again Christians followed through on this responsibility by sharing the gospel at least once over the last year with the hope that the person would come to faith in Jesus Christ as their Savior. The Barna Group reports the not-so-good news that boomers (those born between 1946 and 1964) and busters (now in their thirties and forties) have declined over the years in their practice of sharing their faith. The one major exception, perhaps surprisingly, are those of the millennial generation (approximately eighteen to thirty-four years old), who have had a significant increase in faith-sharing practices (from 56 percent in 2010 to 65 percent in 2013). It is surmised that since the percentage of millennials who are overtly Christian is significantly smaller than the older generations, they are more motivated to make a case for their faith.[33] In another study only 25 percent of believers could affirm the statement that they had "spent time building friendships with non-Christians for the purpose of sharing Christ with them." In addition, only 1 percent of Christ-followers believe they have the gift of evangelism, which reflects the static growth of the church in America.

We must acknowledge that the climate in the Western world makes any traditional form of sharing the gospel more difficult than in the recent past. It can be intimidating to live at a time when the spirit of relativism reigns. Relativism is the belief that there is no absolute truth. The only truth we have is personal truth or what is true for me. This is what I would call designer truth or religion. We each pick and choose from the salad bar of options according to our personal taste. Nothing is right or wrong; what matters is what works for us. Christians can be suspect because we speak of Jesus as *the* truth; he is true for all. We can be readily accused of trying to force our beliefs on others in a culture of maximum choice. Standing for a universal truth can come across as being intolerant and judgmental. When the force of culture is flowing powerfully in one direction, and we are going upstream, it takes deep conviction to not get swept away in the prevailing current. Many times people have pushed back at me with, "You mean to tell me if I don't accept Christ I am going to hell?" Generally, I have swallowed hard and said something to the effect, "If God has made his identity known to all through Jesus Christ, wouldn't you think I should let you know about that?"

In this atmosphere of intimidation, we must ask ourselves what we have to offer. Do we truly believe we have something so vital and life giving that we must give it away? Do we want others to have the same fulfilling relationship with God as we do? Pastor Bill Hybels says that seekers might look at our lives and ask themselves, "If I become a Christian, am I trading up or trading down?" So the question becomes, is our experience of the love and joy of Jesus worth transmitting to others? For many believers, it appears not to be so.

How would you assess both the capacity and willingness of fellow believers to share the good new of Jesus with others? Please respond by using figure 1.7.

Rate the commitment to the church as a covenant community on a scale of 1 to 5, 1 being optional and 5 being essential.		
Discipleship Symptom	**Rating**	**Notes**
Witness: Inactive vs. Active		

Figure 1.7. Inactive versus active

The Discipleship Gap: You Are Here

Is this overview an accurate picture of the state of discipleship today? Is it overly dire? Does this portrait accord with your reality? If this description of the gap between the biblical standard and the current state of discipleship is close to being accurate, then enormous work must be done to close the gap.

My goal in this chapter has been to bring into stark contrast the current state of discipleship. Leaders must speak to this gap. John Kotter in *Leading Change* says that a primary reason why change does not occur is that there is no sense of urgency.[34] Leadership is about instilling urgency. One way urgency is created is by painting a picture of God's intention over against the sober reality we are living in.

When we accurately assess the way things are, we have hope of getting to the way things were designed to be. We have hope because Jesus, the Lord of the church, desires his bride to be without spot and blemish, for his life will be manifest through his church. Barna observes,

> Christianity would be incredibly influential in our culture if Christians consistently lived their faith. Most non-Christians don't read the Bible, so they judge Christianity by the lives of the Christians they see. The problem is that millions of Christians don't live like Christians—and that's partially because they don't know what they believe and therefore cannot apply appropriate scriptural values to their lives.[35]

How have we gotten to this state of discipleship? It is one thing to describe where we are; it is another to identify the root causes of the problem. In chapter two I will complete our portrait of reality by identifying the contributing factors to the current state of discipleship. Only when we know and face the causes of our low level of discipleship can we begin to address them.

2

THE DISCIPLESHIP MALAISE

Getting to the Root Causes

I began this book with my *aha* discovery of the power of microgroups. Let me balance that with my *duh* moment, which became equally revelatory. You might recall those times when a truth was right before your eyes but you didn't see it, and later it came into focus and you said, "Duh."

I was pastoring a church in the Silicon Valley of Northern California at a time when mission statements were the craze. Stephen Covey had just published his bestseller *Seven Habits of Highly Effective People* (1989). According to Covey, one of the habits of effective people is that they write and stay focused on a personal mission statement. His advice was to focus every day with the end in mind. Mission statements carried over to the business world. A crisp, succinct mission statement is designed to remind the enterprise of exactly what business they are in. For example, when you read Starbucks' mission statement, "To inspire and nurture the human spirit—one person, one cup and one neighborhood at a time," you readily acknowledge that they know what business they are in.

Since the church I was pastoring had no written mission statement, we succumbed to the pressure of the moment and set about creating one. I conscripted "volunteers" from our elder board to work with me on the draft. In retrospect, it was the blind leading the blind. None of us had any clear picture of what this should look like when we were done. We wrote draft after draft. Each successive version was brought to the elder board with a ho-hum response. Finally, out of sheer exhaustion and fear that we would deforest much of Northern California with all the paper we were consuming, the board finally agreed to adopt something.

Shortly after all this work, I had my *duh* revelation. I suddenly realized that Jesus had done all the work for us. Jesus had given the same mission statement to every church when he said, "Go and make disciples of all nations." Sure, we may take Jesus' imperative and put it into our own freshly worded statement, but we don't need to grope around to find what we are to be about. When this hit me, it was as if Jesus said to me, "Keep a laser focus on this mission. Don't take your eyes off of it. And do what you can to ensure that making disciples is the central focus."

This chapter looks at the root causes that have created the superficial state of discipleship, which we explored in chapter one. Underlying all the particulars about the causes of our discipleship malaise, which I highlight in this chapter, the issue of losing focus on the main thing is the root cause. I was living in the fog of the busy life of a pastor, trying to keep all the plates spinning that come with this responsibility. When the fog lifted I heard: Keep the main thing, the main thing.

C. S. Lewis has stated the main thing in a most powerful way:

> The church exists for nothing else but to draw men into Christ, to make them little Christs. If they are not doing that, all the cathedrals, clergy, missions, sermons, even the Bible itself, are simply a waste of time. God became Man for no other purpose. It is even doubtful, you know, whether the whole universe was created for any other purpose.[1]

So what gets us off the main thing? How do we get sidetracked? We will explore eight distractions from producing disciples of Jesus:

- Diversion from Primary Calling
- Discipling Through Programs
- Reducing the Christian Life
- A Two-Tiered Understanding of Discipleship
- Unwillingness to Call People to Discipleship
- An Inadequate View of the Church

- No Clear Pathway to Maturity
- Lack of Personal Discipling

Diversion from Primary Calling

The first cause of the low estate of discipleship is that pastors have been diverted from their primary calling to "equip the saints for the work of ministry."

The New Testament does not give an extended job description for the role that pastors and elders are to play vis-à-vis the whole people of God, but what we are given is clear. The nearest thing to a pastoral job description is found in the oft-quoted Ephesians 4:12, which says that those given to the church as its leaders are "to equip the saints for the work of ministry." In my book *Unfinished Business* there is an extended exploration of the meaning of the term *equip*.[2] Leaders in the church have been assigned the task of preparing, training or discipling ordinary believers, referred to as saints, for their place of service in the body of Christ. D. Elton Trueblood captures Paul's intent: "The ministry is for all who share in Christ's life, the pastorate is for those who possess the peculiar gift of being able to help other men and women to practice any ministry to which they are called."[3] If the equippers are performing their role, a whole series of dominoes fall in sequence: the body of Christ is built up, unity of faith is grounded in the knowledge of God's Son, the church grows to maturity, "fully developed within and without, fully alive like Christ" (Ephesians 4:12-13 *The Message*).

If Satan wanted to disrupt these positives aspects that flow from the ministry leaders' focus on equipping the saints, what would he do? He would do what has actually occurred—divert the leaders from fulfilling their God-given function of equipping the saints. Instead of equipping the saints to do the work of ministry, those in pastoral leadership do it themselves.

The consistent pushback I receive when I challenge pastors to make relational disciple making central to their ministry is that they are already too busy. You want me to add this to my already full agenda? Where would I find time for this? A pastor of a megachurch was invited to join twelve other pastors of large churches to meet with one of the nation's best known and highly respected pastors at his church facility. This was to be a time of resourcing each other, so they generated the topics of interest. Once the twenty-plus topics were listed, they prioritized the list for discussion. The topic of interest to the pastor in question was: How can we best form people spiritually? This was just another way of saying: How do we grow disciples? Since no one else seemed interested in this question, his topic came out dead last in the priority list. Thus, it got only thirty minutes of a two-day agenda, while the others were already mentally packing to head to the airport.

Their focus was on everything but intentional disciple making. When it came to this final topic, the convener readily admitted: "As you can see, I left this topic for last. The reason is that I don't know what to do about this subject. In this day and age, how does a church significantly help people in spiritual formation? If you can get your people to worship, do outreach and volunteer weekly in a ministry, that's about the best you can do." One pastor in this gathering admitted that they had no mechanism to move people spiritually from one place to the next. "We have absolutely no vehicle for getting our people from spiritual immaturity to maturity. We do not equip them. In fact, we cannot."[4]

Pastors have been consumed by pastoral care. Assigning caregiving to the professionals has had a disastrous impact on people's ability to grow into adulthood in the faith. When someone is in the hospital, grieving the loss of a loved one, dealing with a marital crisis or experiencing the pain of a rebellious child, the pastor is expected to be present. We have honed an interlocking set of expectations from people to pastor that comes in the form of an emotional contract: "If I am having difficulty, pastor, I expect you to be there to get me through it. If you don't show up, you are failing to do your job. If you have failed in providing care, you have failed as a pastor."

Scripture actually gives us a case study of how the apostles handled caregiving expectations. A dispute arose in the Jerusalem church because the Greek-speaking widows felt they "were being overlooked in the daily distribution of food," when compared to the Hebrew-speaking widows. The problem was brought to the apostles for a solution. In their wisdom they decided, "It would not be right for us to neglect the ministry of the word of God in order to wait on tables" (Acts 6:1-2 NIV). Apparently one of the solutions proposed was that the apostles should add serving the widows to their job description. After all, what better way to show your servant spirit than to care for widows, who are at the center of our Lord's heart? They saw this solution as the temptation that it was. They could easily be distracted from their call to the ministry of the Word and prayer. In fact, their eventual solution expanded ministry by creating an opportunity for seven Greek-speaking men "full of the Spirit and wisdom" (Acts 6:3 NIV) to be added to the ministry force.[5]

To the extent that pastors overperform by assuming responsibilities given to the whole body of Christ, the ministry of the people of God is undermined. We have created a system in which we pay pastors to do ministry and the people are the recipients of the pastors' care. I call this the "dependency model of ministry." Instead, we need to move to an *equipping model* of ministry. In order to picture this, Trueblood suggests that we need a new image of the pastor as equipper, which redefines the relationship between pastor and people. Trueblood suggests that "player-coach" is the best modern image for a pastor, for it is the glory of the coach to help team members discover, develop and be deployed to play their parts on the team (the body of Christ). By emphasizing *player-coach* we are reminded that we don't have separate clergy teams and laity teams, but we are all a part of the same team, accomplishing together the mission of growing disciples of Jesus.[6]

Discipling Through Programs

The second cause of the low estate of discipleship is that we have tried to make disciples through programs.

The scriptural model for growing disciples is through relationships. Jesus called the Twelve to "be with him" (Mark 3:14), for their lives would be transformed through personal association. Proximity produces disciples. The apostle Paul also had his ministry partners (for example, Timothy). In this side-by-side ministry, leaders could be trained to carry on after his departure. Disciples are made in intentional relationships—"iron sharpens iron" (Proverbs 27:17).

In today's church we have replaced person-centered growth with programs as the means of making disciples. By programs I mean the structured group methods we use to herd large groups of people through systems. Examples of programs are age-graded Sunday schools, adult education classes, needs-based seminars, small-groups or even highly structured discipleship programs.

Though these programs can contribute to discipleship development, they miss the central ingredient in discipleship. Each disciple is a unique individual with growth factors particular to him or her. Unless people receive personal attention so that their precise growth needs are addressed in a way that calls them to die to self and live fully to Christ, disciples will not be formed.

Since individual, personal investment is costly and time intensive, we have substituted programs to streamline the process. George Barna says programs

> are often embraced as a way of organizing large groups of people into an orderly process that can be easily managed and controlled. If we were to be honest, we would have to admit that the absence of real measures of personal growth are a testimony to our concern about style more than substance, and our commitment to taking action more than having impact.[7]

In other words, programs can make it look like we are growing disciples, but that is more of an illusion than reality, and we know it.

Why don't programs make disciples? As I see it, programs have four common characteristics.

Programs tend to be information- or knowledge-based. Programs operate on the assumption that if someone has more information, that information will automatically lead to transformation. In other words, right knowledge produces right living. John Ortberg has mused over the fact that two people can hold to the same doctrinal beliefs and yet be wildly different in terms of their behavior. One person can be loving, kind, gentle and gracious, whereas another can be judgmental, rigid, brittle and prickly. They both believe the same things. What makes the difference? Far more than their theological or biblical knowledge.

As one who has been a pastor and a professor, I am certainly not opposed to acquiring knowledge. But information alone does not lead to transformation. We can hold truth in a compartmentalized fashion without having it change the way we think, feel or act. James made the same observation when he said that faith apart from works is dead. We can subscribe to a set of beliefs without allowing them to affect our lifestyle. To drive home his point James writes, "Even the demons believe [in God]—and shudder" (James 2:19). We tend to view the teaching process like this: the teacher with the full pitcher empties its contents into the student's empty pitcher. It is simply a process of information transfer. Since Christlikeness is our goal, we must ask whether more information by itself accomplishes that.

Programs are the one preparing for the many. Most programs are built around an individual or a few people who do the hard work of preparation. The rest come, to a greater or lesser degree, as passive recipients. Though this may provide tremendous benefit to those who have done the preparation, the result is usually enormous amounts of unprocessed information for the participants. The obvious example of this is preaching. As much as I believe in the power of preaching for conviction and decision, I would be naive to believe that preaching alone produces disciples. If preaching could have produced disciples, the job of making disciples would have been done a long time ago. (See chapter ten for a much more complete discussion of the role of preaching in making disciples.)

During my time as a seminary professor, I had the opportunity to sit in a congregation as a worshiper. This allowed time to reflect on what happens or doesn't happen in this setting. I have concluded that the preached Word needs the context of community, where its meaning can be discussed and its implications considered. To the extent that we listen to preaching week after week without processing it, our spirits can build a resistance to it. Only as we wrestle with the Word, particularly in a relational setting, does it seep into our being and transform us.

Programs are characterized by regimentation or synchronization. The nature of most programs is that they do not take into account an individual's growth rate or the issues he or she is facing, which is essential to growing disciples. When more than five people gather, a system must be set up in which people are required to move through content in lockstep fashion. So we have programs of some specified length of time designed to make disciples. Thus, people cover identical content in the same sequence at the same rate, and completing the program is equated with making disciples.

This conjures up images of mass production. We attempt to make disciples in the same way we construct a car. When the process is completed, disciples are supposed to pop out of the other end of the production line. But regimentation and synchronization are counterproductive to disciple making. Every individual is unique. Making a disciple requires a customized approach. This means that a person's knowledge, growth in character, personal challenges, discernment of unique ministry identity, and obedience in thought, word and deed need to be dealt with in the context of Jesus' radical and total claim on his or her life in a community setting. Barna concludes, "Few churches intentionally guide their people through a strategic learning and developmental process that has been customized for the student."[8]

Programs generally have low personal accountability. How many of us have someone to hold us accountable to our obedience to Jesus Christ? Programs of discipleship often give the illusion of accountability. But on closer examination the focus is on completing the assigned curriculum rather than committing to life change. Barna observes, "Few churches have systems by which they measure what is happening in the life of church adherents. Few believers have lined up a trustworthy and competent partner who will hold them accountable to specific and measurable goals."[9]

Though all approaches to disciple making will have programmatic elements, such as structure and curriculum (even if it is the Bible), the individual's growth is always preeminent in a relational setting.

Reducing the Christian Life

The third cause of the low estate of discipleship is that we have reduced the gospel to the eternal benefits we get from Jesus, rather than living as his students.

When we consider the superficial state of discipleship, shouldn't we see if there is something wrong with the terms we have been using to present the gospel? Dallas Willard writes, "Should we not at least consider the possibility that this poor result is not in spite of what we teach and how we teach, but precisely because of it?"[10] What is the gospel that has led to nondiscipleship? One that is focused on the benefits we get from Jesus. This is what Willard has sarcastically called "barcode" Christianity. All we are interested in is getting rung up by the great scanner in the sky. I have dubbed this the "transactional gospel." It's a transaction because we see the message of salvation in accounting terms: our sin is entered as an eternal debit on our account; Jesus' death on the cross is our full payment for our sin; by faith his credit is transferred to our account, which cancels our debt. We are handed a receipt stamped "Paid in Full." Forgiveness of our sin debt and the assurance of eternal life is the gospel. Period.

John Ortberg says that we are preaching the gospel of minimal entrance requirements to get into heaven when we die. He notes that in the New Testament there is a natural progression as people move toward Jesus. People start out as *strangers* to Jesus. They then move from *strangers* to *admirers*.[11] For example, Zacchaeus, a tax collector, was far from Jesus, but he heard enough of Jesus' reputation to climb a tree in order to get a glimpse of this intriguing man. He had gone from *stranger* to *admirer*, something neither Pilate nor Herod ever did. From an admirer Zacchaeus became a *follower* when Jesus invited himself to be a guest in his home. But Ortberg adds the stunning suggestion that we have added a category in our day between *admirer* and *follower*. We have inserted *user* of Jesus. The gospel we have been communicating suggests that we *use* Jesus to get into heaven when we die. This gospel that focuses on the benefits we receive from Jesus has no direct connection to being a follower of Jesus.

How else do we account for the disjunction between professed faith and the quality of our discipleship? Willard says, "The most telling thing about the contemporary Christian is that he or she simply has no compelling sense that understanding of and conformity with the clear teachings of Christ is of any vital importance to his or her life, and certainly not that it is in any way essential."[12] We have transformed the gospel into the benefits we receive from Jesus rather than the call to be conformed to the life of Jesus. We want abundance without obedience.

A Two-Tiered Understanding of Discipleship

The fourth cause of the low estate of discipleship is that we have made discipleship for super-Christians, not ordinary believers.

There appears to be a two-tiered understanding of what it mean to be a Christian. Michael Wilkins, a professor at Talbot School of Theology, regularly asks two questions when he speaks to groups about discipleship. The contrasting answers to these questions give us insight into the way people understand discipleship. The first question is, "How many of you can say in the humble confidence of your own heart that you are a true disciple of Jesus? Please raise your hand." The usual response is that a few hesitant people raise their hands shoulder high while looking to see who is raising their hands. Then they put them down quickly. Then Wilkins proceeds to the second question: "How many of you can say in the humble confidence of your own heart that you are a true Christian? Please raise your hand." Immediately most hands jet straight up, without hesitation.[13]

Why can people affirm being true Christians but are hesitant to identify themselves as true disciples of Jesus? The primary difference, I believe, is the angle from which we approach both labels. In many people's minds, being a Christian is about what Christ has done for us; whereas a disciple is about what we are doing for Christ. *Christian* is a noun; *disciple* is a verb. To be a Christian is passive; to be a disciple is active. To be a Christian means "I get in on the benefits plan"; to be a disciple means "I have to pay a price."

The elephant in the room in many churches is the unstated assumption that a person can be a Christian without being a disciple. We have made an uneasy peace with this distinction. We have lowered our expectations. Church leaders expect only a relatively small percentage of people to "get it" and become disciples. So we reserve the category of discipleship for the unusual layperson who seems to understand that being a disciple encompasses all dimensions of life. In addition, there are those who respond to God's call to be a pastor, missionary or parachurch worker. We celebrate these people because they have devoted their whole life to following Jesus.

Biblical discipleship does not allow for two classes of followers: the ordinary and extraordinary, Christian and disciple. There are Christians who have not lived up to the expectations of a disciple yet can still be called

Christians, but that in no way lets them off the hook. Paul refers to Christians who have not progressed as babes in Christ who are still drinking milk when they should be taking solid food (1 Corinthians 3:1-3). This is a far cry from our present state of having first-class and second-class disciples.

We need to recapture the biblical expectation defined by Jesus. "Then he said to them all, 'Whoever wants to be my disciple must deny themselves and take up their cross daily and follow me'" (Luke 9:23 NIV). This was Jesus' starting point. He did not have a tiered ranking of disciples, but the same standard for all.

Unwillingness to Call People to Discipleship

The fifth cause of the low estate of discipleship is that leaders have been unwilling to call people to discipleship.

David Platt, Francis Chan, Shane Clairborne and Kyle Idleman have been dubbed the "young radicals" who are calling the church to face again the costly call of following Christ.[14] Echoing Dietrich Bonhoeffer's famous line from *The Cost of Discipleship*, "When Christ calls a man, he bids him come and die," they are taking on the comfortable American version of cushy Christianity. They raise the question, Why aren't we willing to lay out the terms of discipleship as Jesus did when he said, "Whoever wants to be my disciple *must* deny themselves and take up their cross daily and follow me" (Luke 9:23 NIV).

So let's get very personal. Why does intentional disciple making frighten us? For some, it is just too time intensive. We know what it will take. We will have to invest in a few lives on a regular basis, which takes time. When we look at all the things on our to-do list as pastors and leaders, where will we fit it? We might think, *This is why parachurch organizations like Navigators, CRU, InterVarsity and the like are needed. They can specialize in discipleship.* We have to maintain congregations, elders, deacons, facilities, budgets, weddings, funerals, a plethora of committees and so forth. Frankly, intentional discipling seems like a luxury. When a leader looks at how long it takes to grow disciples intentionally, there is not enough short-term fruit to show for it. Leaders get rewarded for the three Bs: budgets, buildings and butts in the seats. Growing a network of invisible disciples is not a criterion on the annual job review.

But perhaps these presenting reasons pale in comparison to the real underlying issue. We live in a consumer culture. The message from the church-growth world is that we need seeker-friendly churches that speak to the felt needs of worldly people. We need to be a hospitable place that puts on an attractive worship experience in tune with the cultural forms of music, public speaking and theater. The prevailing wisdom has been "lower the obstacles so the gospel can be heard."

In the *Renovation of the Church* Kent Carlson and Mike Lueken tell the story of a church that followed this church-growth advice, and their subsequent attempts to shift the model to intentional disciple making. After years of drawing significant crowds through the seeker-sensitive model, they had a wake-up call. The centerpiece of a staff retreat was Lyle Schaller's book *The Very Large Church*. They zeroed in on a point Schaller did not want them to miss: "The central issue is that consumerism in now a fact of life. . . . Do you identify this new context as a source of despair? Or as a challenge to your creativity?" As the staff explored resigning themselves to the necessity of exploiting consumerism, God met them in an unexpected way. Here was their discovery: "Gradually, we began to get some clarity on a troubling truth: attracting people to church based upon consumer demands is in direct and irredeemable conflict with inviting people, in Jesus' words, to lose their lives in order to find them."[15] This book tells an agonizing story of changing from a consumer-driven church to one intent on forming people into Jesus' disciples. Bottom line: it is costly.

Does being faithful to the mission Jesus calls his church to require more than we are willing to pay?

An Inadequate View of the Church

The sixth cause of the low estate of discipleship is that we have an inadequate view of the church as a discipleship community.

In chapter one I mentioned that many who claim Christ view the church as an option, not a requirement. In order to view the church in this way, one must have an inadequate understanding of the place of the church in God's redemptive plan. Biblically, discipleship is never seen as a Jesus-and-me solo relationship, for the church is a discipleship *community*.

This is Paul's message to the church at Corinth: "You are the body of Christ [corporately] and individually members of it" (1 Corinthians 12:27). Not only is God saving individuals, but he also is forming a people. Our identity as believers is found and shaped in community. Paul strikes a perfect balance between our relationship to the community and our identity as individuals. In the church our individuality is maintained. We are not drops of water consumed by the ocean. At the same time we don't have an individual identity apart from the church. Our value as believers is known by playing our God-assigned role in building up the church through our spiritual gifts. The Christian life is inherently communal.

If it seems like I am speaking a foreign language, it is because I am. As we noted in the last section, people are driven by their consumer needs and desires. Another aspect of the same malady is radical individualism. Though this is a prized American value—after all, it is the basis for the initiative and inventiveness of an entrepreneurial spirit—it does not provide the basis for communal cohesion and inculcation of shared values. Dallas Willard describes the triumph of individualism, "Individual desire has come to be the standard and rule of everything."[16] A discipleship community needs shared beliefs, values and norms, which are reinforced through mutual accountability.

I am a part of the baby boomer generation, which has been in the forefront of propounding the gospel of self-fulfillment and self-actualization. The self is what counts. Is it any wonder that the parents of my generation have passed on this version of faith to their children? The National Study of Youth and Religion conducted from 2003 to 2005 focused on the faith of teens thirteen to seventeen years old. Their summary label for the nature of adolescent spirituality is "moralistic therapeutic deism." Two of the five tenets of this faith are "the central goal in life is to be happy and feel good about oneself" and "God is not involved in my life except when I need to resolve a problem."[17] In short, be good, feel good and check in with God when we have a need. "Moralistic Therapeutic Deism makes no pretense at changing lives; it is low commitment, compartmentalized set of attitudes aimed at 'meeting my needs' and 'making me happy' rather than bending my life in a pattern of love and obedience to God."[18]

In what should be a wake-up call for evangelicals, Mormon teenagers in this study demonstrated the highest congruence between their beliefs and practice. They were the least likely to engage in high-risk behavior and were consistently the most positive, healthy, hopeful and self-aware teens. In other words, they are spiritually formed in a cohesive community based on routines of education and service, and rooted in the family, church and mission that seamlessly flow together. Though most Christians would not want to adopt Mormon theology, there is much about their practice of disciple making as community that we should want to borrow.

The church has allowed individualized faith to undermine the tight-knit community necessary for disciples to be formed. Jesus said that our love for one another (John 13:34-35) and our visible unity (John 17:20-23) would be signs to the world that we are his disciples and that he was sent from the Father. These qualities need to be at the heart of a disciple-making community. Yet our lack of commitment to covenantal community makes this apologetic only a wistful hope. When I was a member of Rotary International, I knew that if I missed four meetings in a row I would be dropped from membership. I would dare say that the disciple-making mission of the church of Jesus Christ far outstrips the mission of Rotary, yet we tend not to have comparable expectations. Given our weak understanding of the church as community, how can we create a culture in which the norm is to become fully devoted followers of Christ?

No Clear Pathway to Maturity

The seventh cause of the low estate of discipleship is that most churches have no clear, public pathway to maturity.

If making disciples is the primary mission of the church, wouldn't we expect most churches to have some public pathway to maturity in Christ? What if a new person came to your church and was eager to grow in his or her faith? The person asks you, "How do I become a fully devoted follower of Christ here?" Would you have an answer? Yet it is rare to find a church with a well-thought-out, easy-to-grasp process or pathway people can take to grow to maturity. In the latest data on the state of discipleship, church leaders were asked if they could improve one thing related to making disciples, what would it be. The number one answer was "develop a more clearly articulated plan or approach to discipleship."[19]

Saddleback Community Church in Southern California has developed the most popular and copied public discipleship model, which they call the Christian Life and Service Seminars (C.L.A.S.S.) or Life Development Process. This process is pictured in the recognizable form of a baseball diamond. Adaptations of this scheme can be found in many churches. On first base, "Discover our Church Family" (Class 101), a person learns about the Saddleback story and how to have a saving relationship with Christ. On second base, "Discover My Spiritual Growth" (Class 201), a person learns basic spiritual disciplines for growth. On third base, "Discover My S.H.A.P.E." (Class 301), a person discovers that their place in ministry is based on their Spiritual gifts, Heart, Abilities, Personality and life Experience. At home plate, "Discover My Life Mission" (Class 401), a person explores their life mission based in compassionate service, and how to share their faith in order to bring another to a saving relationship with Jesus Christ. The pitcher's mound at the center of the baseball diamond is *worship*.

Though this model has been criticized as simplistic because it does not recognize life's setbacks or perhaps the need for a far more relational emphasis, its genius is that it is a quickly graspable, progressive image of what it means to move more deeply into the life of following Jesus. Rick Warren states, "Instead of growing a church with programs, focus on growing people with a process. We need a process to go with purpose. Unless the purpose is fleshed out in a process, then we don't have anything but nice platitudes."[20] The church, says Warren, needs to clearly define its purposes and then organize around them so there is a sequential process to accomplish them in the lives of believers.

"How can I become a faithful disciple of Christ?" was in the forefront of my mind throughout my tenure in my last pastorate. We started with that end in mind, asking the question that dominates chapter eight of this book. What environment creates the transformative setting that fosters accelerated growth to maturity in Christ? We concluded that we wanted people to find their way into microgroups. So our motto was that we were "majoring in microgroups." Starting there, we worked backwards, trying to envision how we could best move people from worship to midsize and small-group community on the way to the destination of microgroups. We knew that once we got people into microgroups, much of what they offered in classes would be covered intensively in an open, relational environment. Yet to underscore Saddleback's insight: couple purpose with a process.[21]

This clarity of purpose and connection to process are missing in most churches. Barna's research concludes,

> Relatively small numbers of born again adults said that their churches give them the specific paths to follow to foster growth. Slightly less than half said their churches had identified any spiritual goals, standards or expectations for the congregation in the past year. . . . Only one out of every five believers stated that their church has some means of facilitating an evaluation of the spiritual maturity or commitment to maturity of their congregation.[22]

This conclusion was supported in the latest findings, for only 1 percent of church leaders said that they were doing "very well" in "discipling new and young believers."[23] However, nine out of ten believers in this same survey said they would take seriously their church's recommendation to pursue a spiritual path if one was presented to them.

Lack of Personal Discipling

The eighth and final cause of the low estate of discipleship, and likely the most telling, is that most Christians have never been personally discipled.

We now come to the burden at the heart of this book. A couple of decades ago Joel Barker wrote a business book in which he introduced what he calls the paradigm shift question: "What is impossible to do in your business [church or ministry], but if it could be done, would fundamentally change it?"[24] In other words, if you could crack it, what is that tough nut that when cracked would be the breakthrough that changes everything? Here is my suggestion for the paradigm shift question: How can we grow Christians into self-initiating, reproducing, fully devoted followers of Jesus Christ? My answer is: The primary way people grow into self-initiating, reproducing, fully devoted followers of Jesus Christ is by being engaged in highly accountable, relational, multiplying discipleship units of three or four (microgroups).

A major reason for the eight flaws in the life of the Christian church is that people have not been personally discipled. By *discipling* I mean "a process that takes place within accountable relationships over a period of time for the purpose of bringing believers to spiritual maturity in Christ."[25] Over the last three decades that I have been conducting workshops on discipleship, I have asked thousands of believers, "How many of you have been in an intentional discipleship relationship in which someone has walked with you over time with the express purpose of helping you become mature in Christ?" Approximately 10 to 15 percent of the people raise their hands. This is probably an unusually high percentage in comparison with the ordinary church population. After all, those at a seminar on discipling have already demonstrated that they are a part of the 20 percent involved in the church community.

I contend that a necessary and pivotal element in providing the motivation and discipline to grow self-initiating, reproducing, fully devoted followers of Jesus comes only through personal investment. The motivation and discipline will not ultimately occur through listening to sermons, sitting in a class, participating in a fellowship group, attending a study group in the workplace or being a member of a small group, but rather in the context of highly accountable, relationally transparent, truth-centered, small (three or four people) discipleship units. In my experience this is the optimum context for transformation. If every believer had this opportunity, we would go a long way toward addressing the causes of the discipleship malaise sketched in this chapter. Barna comments on this as well: "A majority (55%) of the adults who indicated their interest in hearing advice on how to improve their spiritual life also said that if the church matched them with a spiritual mentor or coach, they would be more likely to pursue the changes suggested to them."[26]

When the results of our church ministries are so different from what Jesus commanded, we must stop and ask, Where have we gone wrong? If the picture I have painted is close to reality, it should cause us to shudder and weep. We must plead to the One who gave us our marching orders and ask, "Lord, how can we get back on track to making quality disciples, which you said is our mission?"

Before going on, take a few minutes to do your reality assessment. Examine each of the causes of discipleship deficit in light of your ministry (see fig. 2.1). To each give a numerical rating between 1 and 5, with 1 being completely true and 5 being not true at all.

Causes of Discipleship Deficit	Rating	Notes
Diversion from primary calling		
Discipling through programs		
Reducing the Christian life		
A two-tiered understanding of discipleship		
Unwillingness to call people to discipleship		
An inadequate view of the church		
No clear pathway to maturity		
Lack of personal discipling		

Figure 2.1. Causes of discipleship deficit

The next three chapters review the biblical vision of how disciples are made. In these chapters we will examine how Jesus and Paul made disciples. Here is another way to answer the paradigm shift question: How can we grow Christians into self-initiating, reproducing, fully devoted followers of Jesus Christ? The answer is: Follow the biblical model. We have lost sight of the obvious. Jesus showed us how we are to develop people by his investment in the Twelve over a three-year period. Paul's life ambition was to "present everyone mature," which he also did through personal investment. A generation ago George Orwell wrote, "We have now sunk to a depth at which the restatement of the obvious is the first duty of intelligent men."[27] My hope is that by walking with Jesus and Paul in their disciple-making school, we will own the imperative that we too must do the Lord's work in the Lord's way.

PART TWO

DOING THE LORD'S WORK IN THE LORD'S WAY

The Bible as a Method Book

3

WHY JESUS INVESTED IN A FEW

I remember the phone call quite well. What I didn't know at the time was how much it would change my life. Don was on the other end of the line. He was a seminary student working as an intern at my church during my college years. Don had begun an outreach ministry to junior high students on Wednesday evenings, which he called Campus Club. It had become more successful in a shorter time than he had imagined, because 130 high-energy balls of fire were tearing through the gymnasium and fellowship hall. Reinforcements were urgent. Don set out in desperate search of some equally high-energy college students who could corral this bunch and invest in their lives. I was on his list. "Greg, how would you like to be a part of a team of college students working with junior high kids on Wednesday nights?" That was one of those moments when I didn't know enough to say no. "Sure, great. What do you want me to do?" I said.

I don't recall that the original invitation included a bonus, but a bonus I got. Don would periodically phone to see if we could get together one on one. Often the substantive portion of this time was preceded by swatting balls around the tennis court. Invariably our time would conclude with an extended side-by-side conversation as we sat on the bench courtside. Don would open his Bible and share with me something from the Word that was speaking to his life. What impressed me about Don was his transparency. He didn't hide from me the dark sides of his life, which the Scripture exposed, or the difficulty of making the appropriate changes. He made it clear that being a follower of Jesus wasn't easy but more than worth the cost involved. In those heart-to-heart talks an unspoken message was transferred to me: "If Don wants to follow Jesus, then I want to follow Jesus."

I don't recall whether Don's personal investment in me was influenced by some grand design about how ministry is done or if he intuitively knew that to make a difference in someone's life he had to get close to that person. But whether it was by intention or instinct, Don has served as a model for me as to the way Jesus ministered.

While I was a seminary student I heard Charles Miller, then youth pastor at Lake Avenue Congregational Church in Pasadena, California, use a memorable phrase. He said the Scripture is not only a message book but also a method book. In other words, the Scripture conveys not only the *what* but also the *how*. We tend to look at Scripture as merely containing the content of the gospel and the commensurate lifestyle. But also embedded in the story of the good news is instruction and modeling of the means we are to use to ensure its transmission into the lives of the next generation. My fundamental assumption is that we have less of a message problem today than we do a method problem. We have not been looking to Scripture to show us how people grow to maturity in Christ so they can reproduce.

In this and the next two chapters we will examine the strategy that Jesus and Paul used to transmit the faith from one generation to another. We need to have the biblical perspective clearly in mind. By following the imperative of Scripture, we can work within small discipling units to carefully grow people in the faith and overcome the rampant superficiality of our age. We will discover in the ministries of Jesus and Paul that they staked their fruitfulness on intentional, relational investment in a few. This is the way to ensure the linkage of discipleship from one generation to the next.

Doing the Lord's Work in the Lord's Way

It is estimated that six to nine months into Jesus' public ministry, he selected from a larger group of followers those who would move from the category of disciples to that of apostles. Luke records this event: "Now during those days he [Jesus] went out to the mountain to pray; and he spent the night in prayer to God. And when day came, he called his disciples and chose twelve of them, whom he also named apostles" (Luke 6:12-13).

We could get the impression from reading Mark's account of Jesus' call of the disciples that the call to be apostles occurred during his first encounter with them. Jesus passed by the Sea of Galilee, observed two sets of brothers, Peter and Andrew and James and John, plying their trade—fishing. He walked up to them and without introduction exclaimed, "Follow me and I will make you fish for people" (Mark 1:17). Precipitously they dropped everything and like puppies followed their new master. So mesmerized were they by Jesus' charisma that they laid down their nets after only a moment's exposure. This conjures up images of glassy-eyed, cult-like obedience to a personality-negating guru.

A closer reading of the Gospels indicates that becoming part of Jesus' inner circle progressed through stages. A. B. Bruce, in *The Training of the Twelve*, says that responding to Jesus' selection to be a part of the inner group was the third of three stages in a process.[1]

The first stage is recorded in John's Gospel. Most commentators view our introduction to the first disciples in John 1 as preceding the point where Matthew, Mark and Luke begin their Gospels. John indicates that the initial encounters with Jesus initiated a period of examination. The first disciples were invited by Jesus to check him out to see if he was the Messiah they were looking for. Andrew and an unnamed disciple (most likely John) were introduced to Jesus by means of John the Baptist. As disciples of John the Baptist, they had been prepared to look for the Messiah for whom John prepared the way. John, upon seeing Jesus, exclaimed, "Look, here is the Lamb of God!" (John 1:36). Andrew and John take it upon themselves to follow Jesus. During this investigative stage Jesus invites them to "come and see" (John 1:39). Jesus encourages exposure to him as a way for the disciples to get a glimpse of who he might be. Also included in this time of inquiry are Peter, who is informed by Andrew, "We have found the Messiah" (John 1:41), and Philip, who uses the same phrase with a skeptical Nathanael (likely Bartholomew), "We have found him" (John 1:45).

We are left with the clear notion that those who would later become the Twelve began as inquirers or seekers. They were not at first encounter presented with the decision to "Follow me" but instead "Come and see." There would soon come a time when a decision would have to be made, but first the authenticity and identity of this engaging person would have a chance to leave a growing impression.

It is at the second stage that we pick up the story in Luke 6. Jesus has called together his team of disciples, from whom he is to select an inner core of twelve. This group has been gathered at Jesus' initiative. If stage one allows the inquirers to control the investigation, at stage two Jesus defines the nature of the relationship through a summons that requires a decision: "Follow me" (Matthew 8:22; 19:21; Mark 1:20; 2:14; Luke 9:59; John 1:43). Speaking to the crowds, Jesus says, "If any want to become my followers, let them deny themselves and take up their cross daily and follow me" (Luke 9:23). Jesus provides the shaping influence. The lexical definition of *disciple* (*mathētēs*) "always implies the existence of a personal attachment which shapes the whole life of the one described as *mathētēs*, and which in its particularity, leaves no doubt as to who is deploying the formative power."[2] What we know at this stage is that Jesus had gathered a larger aggregate of followers who had been itinerating with him. The Twelve were a part of this larger assembly. This larger group could have been equivalent to the seventy that Jesus would later send out two by two (Luke 10:1-2).

The third stage moves each of the Twelve from the category of one among many disciples to a leadership role in Jesus' intimate inner circle. In other words, any follower of Jesus is a disciple, but only twelve of these disciples are apostles. Another way to say it is that all apostles are disciples, but not all disciples are apostles. This role is reserved for a chosen few. If stage one is "come and see" and stage two is "follow me," then stage three is "come and be with me."

Against this backdrop, our interest is the strategic import of Jesus' selection of the Twelve and how his focus on a few serves as a model for how we are to grow disciples and, subsequently, leaders.

The selection of the Twelve was evidently a crucial moment in Jesus' ministry. Luke underscores the pivotal nature of this selection by telling us that Jesus spent all night in prayer. So vital was this moment to the future of Jesus' ministry that extended and intense time alone with his Father preceded the call. We can only speculate as to what was on Jesus' heart that night. Was he attempting to discern who should make the final cut? Had Jesus whittled down the list to fifteen and was in a quandary as to which three to eliminate? Probably not. My best guess is that Jesus was not so much trying to settle on the right ones as he was praying that they would become the right ones. Perhaps Jesus projected each of the Twelve on the screen of his imagination, visualizing what they would grow into under his tutelage. Jesus saw these disciples not only as unformed lumps of coal but, under his formative and loving pressure, as the diamonds they would become. Jesus knew full well that Peter would brashly oppose his self-designation as a suffering Messiah and would vehemently deny him. Yet Jesus envisioned by faith that Peter would become the "rock" upon whom he would build his church (Matthew 16:18).

The Strategic Question

Not only does Jesus' all-night prayer raise the level of the strategic significance of the choosing of the Twelve, but so does the manner in which the selection was made. Luke tells us, "He called his disciples [together] and chose twelve of them" (Luke 6:13). In other words, from the larger group Jesus called publicly those who would be part of his inner circle. This reminds me of my elementary school days on the playground; the two most popular kids would serve as the opposing captains for the pickup games. Those of us clamoring to play stood around the two team captains waiting for our names to be called. To hear your name called first made you feel not only special but also a bit arrogant. You could then stand next to the team captain as one of the in crowd and suggest who should be chosen next. By making his selection process a public event, Jesus potentially set up a dynamic in which a few felt special and the rest felt left out. Why would Jesus create an atmosphere that would foster jealousy on the part of those not chosen and potential pride in those who were?

I hear objections from pastors who say they can't choose a few to invest in because they will be accused of having favorites. If the pastor spends more time with a few, a buzz spreads throughout the church that the pastor has his or her inner circle. From the congregation's perspective the pastor must be equally available to all. These suspicions are rooted in two assumptions. First, the pastor's primary role after preaching is to be a caregiver. Ministry is equated with taking care of the needs of the flock. To the shepherd, all the sheep must be equally valuable.

The second assumption revolves around an appropriate concern about the abuse of power. A perception can grow within a congregation that a small group controls what happens in the life of a church or ministry. Church members may then see themselves as outsiders, finding it difficult to penetrate the invisible barrier of an undetectable inner circle. The egalitarian model of equal access, however, is rooted in a fundamental misunderstanding of the pastoral role. In the biblical view, pastors are gifted leaders who are to equip the saints for ministry, not to minister in place of the saints. Jesus thought that investing in a few was so important that he made the selection process public, even at the risk of stirring up jealousy and pride.

What was so important about having a few in his inner circle that Jesus was willing to risk the dynamics of jealousy? What were the strategic reasons behind this selection of the Twelve to be his intimate associates? Of the many valid reasons for Jesus' investment in a few, two seem most directly related to Jesus' goal of making self-initiating, reproducing, fully devoted followers: internalization and multiplication.

Internalization

The only way for Jesus to (1) help flawed and faithless common people grow into mature disciples and (2) make sure that his kingdom would transcend his earthly ministry was to have a core group who knew in-depth his person and mission. His life and mission needed to be internalized in the lives of the disciples.[3] The way to ensure that they internalized his mission was through "purposeful proximity."[4]

But, we might object, *if Jesus was trying to reach as many as possible, why not allow the crowds and his popularity to grow so that the entourage became a mass movement?* Jesus was so popular that the religious leaders dared not arrest him in public. There were times when the crush of the crowds so threatened his well being that he needed to get into a boat and address the people from just off shore. Why not stake his future on his popularity?

In fact, we see in Jesus a healthy and appropriate skepticism of the masses. Jesus was well aware of the crowd's ignoble motives for following him. John gives an insight into Jesus' understanding of human nature: "When he [Jesus] was in Jerusalem during the Passover festival, many believed in his name because they saw the signs that he was doing. But Jesus on his part would not entrust himself to them, because he knew all people and needed no one to testify about anyone; for he himself knew what was in everyone" (John 2:23-25). The implication of John's words is that people will flock to demonstrations of power, especially if they are the beneficiaries of that power. The desperate came and received healing. Others came to be around the miracle worker. Like moths attracted to light, people are fascinated and feel alive in the presence of a charismatic, life-giving figure. Yet Jesus knew that those who clamored to be near were fickle. As soon as the demands of discipleship were articulated, his fan club would dwindle.

The very nature of a crowd is the ability to be lost in it. It costs nothing to be a part of the masses. One can either be positively or negatively inclined. A member of a crowd, such as a worshiper in a congregation, can remain lost in the sea of faces, neither having to commit nor declare loyalty. Someone in a crowd can be anything from a curious observer to a skeptic or bored pew sitter. Jesus ministered to the crowd in order to call people out of it. A person is not on the road to discipleship unless he or she comes out of the crowd to identify with Jesus. There are twin prerequisites for following Christ—cost and commitment, neither of which can occur in the anonymity of the masses.

What would have been the outcome if Jesus had staked the future of his ministry on the loyalty of the crowds? We know the answer because we are given a window into the dramatic turnaround of the populace. Jesus' public popularity reached a crescendo on the day we call Palm Sunday. He rode into Jerusalem amid the adoration of those waiting for their military messiah. Coats and palm branches created a pathway on which Jesus' donkey trod. The city was filled with shouts of "Hosanna, glory to God in the highest!" Yet in five days some of those same mouths would howl, "Crucify him, crucify him!" This turning away is why A. B. Bruce wrote, "But for the twelve, the doctrine, the works, the image of Jesus might have perished from human resemblance, nothing remaining but a vague mythical tradition, of historical value, of little practical importance."[5]

In spite of Jesus' clear strategy of calling people from the crowds and focusing on a few, we continue to rely on preaching and programs as the means to make disciples. If we rely on the teaching content of preaching to fuel discipleship, then we have a misplaced confidence. Discipleship is fundamentally a relational process. Preaching can be a solitary one. The worshiper tends to be an isolated, passive recipient of the preached word. Preaching at its best calls people to become a disciple by pointing people to disciple-making settings, such as reproducible, discipling relationships.

In addition to preaching, as I indicated in chapter one, we have relied on programs to make disciples. We rely on programs because we don't want to pay the price of personal investment that discipleship requires. By putting people through programs, we foolishly hope that we can mass-produce disciples. Leroy Eims critiques this approach incisively, "Disciples cannot be mass produced. We cannot drop people into a program and see disciples emerge at the end of the production line. It takes time to make disciples. It takes individual personal attention."[6]

Jesus knew that he had to get beyond the superficial and prioritize a few if disciples were to be made. This required that his disciples have consistent, continuous exposure to his life so he could speak to the real stuff of their lives in the context of honest and open interchange. When the disciples argued over who was the greatest, he was able to turn their value system on its head by insisting that in his kingdom the greatest are the least. Peter revealed his working model of a messiah when he told Jesus that no messiah of his was going to die at the hands of the religious leaders. Jesus immediately rebuked Peter for being nothing less than the mouthpiece of Satan. On numerous occasions Jesus' public teaching was followed by a private tutorial for the disciples. The disciples had the opportunity to ask for an explanation of the meaning of Jesus' words, and Jesus had the opportunity to speak to the implications for their lives in a way that could never be conveyed to the crowds.

I have often wondered why Jesus didn't employ the usual means of preserving his legacy. We have nothing penned by his hand. He seemed unconcerned about official manuscripts or enlisting a scribe who could record all of his teachings. It is standard practice that when presidents leave office, they open a presidential library to preserve and display the significant documents and media moments from their administration. A former president attempts to shape the perceptions of history by writing his memoirs. Why did Jesus not choose the same approach? Jesus appeared to rely on two means to carry his life and mission forward: the Holy Spirit and the Twelve. His life was transferred to their lives by his Spirit and by his association with and investment in them. The irrefutable legacy Jesus wanted to leave behind was the transformed lives of ordinary men who would carry on his work after he returned to the Father. Internalization occurred through intense association.

Bruce concludes, "This careful, painstaking education of the disciples secured [that] the teacher's influence should be permanent; that His kingdom should be founded on deep and indestructible convictions in the minds of a few, not on the shifting sands of *superficial* impressions in the minds of the many."[7]

The first strategic reason for Jesus' focus on a few was to ensure the *internalization* of his life and ministry in those who would be the foundation of the Jesus movement.

Multiplication

With Jesus' focus on the Twelve, one might conclude that he was unconcerned about the multitudes. Jim Egli and Paul Zehr, in their study of the Gospel of Mark, found that Jesus spent 49 percent of his time with the disciples, and even more time as he set his face toward Jerusalem and the cross.[8] Is this further evidence that the masses were receding from his field of vision? Absolutely not! Jesus did not think like we do. We think we need to put on events that draw crowds to reach the multitudes. We equate vision with the size of our audience. Jesus had vision of another sort. He had enough vision to think small. Indeed, it was because of his compassion for the harassed and harried throng that Jesus gave himself to the Twelve. Eugene Peterson's humorous overstatement puts this in perspective: "Jesus, it must be remembered, restricted nine-tenths of his ministry to twelve Jews because it was the only way to redeem all Americans (fill in whatever ethnic group)."[9]

The irony is that in our attempt to reach the masses through mass means we have failed to train people the masses could emulate. We often perpetuate superficiality by casting a wider net without the commensurate depth. Jesus multiplied his life in the Twelve so there would be more of himself to go around. In the mid-1970s the movie *Jesus Christ Superstar* stirred controversy because of its portrayal of a very human Christ confused about his mission. While the theology of the film left much to be desired, one powerful scene left a deep impression on me. In this scene Jesus is a solitary figure standing on the slope of barren, scraggly desert hillside. As he sings a song of pathos, black slinky figures emerge from the pockmarked crevices. Each figure represents an aspect of the world's darkness. As the Christ figure sings emotively about humanity's inhumanity, crushing poverty, incurable disease and the great enemy death, these black slithery beings envelop Jesus one at a time until he is crushed and covered by the darkness. The viewer is left with the question, How can one person take on and bear all of this darkness alone? Of course, on the most fundamental level we believe that Jesus did bear it all as the solitary substitute for the guilt of our sin through his death on the cross. Yet there is a sense in which Jesus did not intend to bear it all. By investing in a few, Jesus intended to transfer his life to others so they would participate in extending his redemptive life to the multitudes.

Robert Coleman writes, "The initial objective of Jesus' plan was to enlist men who could bear witness to his life and carry on His work after He returned to His father."[10]

George Martin takes Jesus' strategy and challenges pastors to apply it to the way they think about ministry today:

> Perhaps today's pastor should imagine that they are going to have three more years in their parish (church) as pastor—that there will be no replacement for them when they leave. If they acted as if this were going to happen, they would put the highest priority on selecting, motivating, and training lay leaders that could carry on as much as possible the mission of the parish after they left. The results of three sustained years of such an approach would be significant. Even revolutionary.[11]

As a part of my workshop on discipleship, I enjoy a playful exercise in which I invite the participants to implement Martin's challenge. Generally 80 to 90 percent of the participants are key lay leaders in their congregation, with the paid staff scattered among them. Their assignment is to rewrite the job descriptions of the paid staff, knowing that they had only three years left in their ministry and no one to replace them. I say, "Here's your chance. You have always wanted to tell your pastors what to do." The lay leaders' responses are perceptive. They realize there must be a radical shift in priorities. There are many things their paid staff must cease doing if they are to leave behind self-initiating, reproducing, fully devoted followers of Jesus. Usually the list of things that others could do includes caregiving responsibilities, various aspects of administration and attendance at committee meetings. In place of these unfocused activities could be intentional discipling relationships; specific leadership training on topics such as preaching, spiritual oversight, evangelism and small group leadership; and careful study of the Word, so that teaching could be in greater depth.

Jesus lived with the urgency of the three-year timeline. With the cross before him, he knew that he had to prepare the Twelve to carry on his mission. Each day meant he was closer to the reason for which he came to this earth, and therefore a day closer to the time when his ministry would become theirs. Jesus' strategy was to expand the leadership base so that instead of there being one of him, there would be twelve (knowing even that one of them would be lost). Mark's account of the selection of the Twelve makes it clear that Jesus intended his ministry to become theirs. "He went up the mountain and called to him those whom he wanted, and they came to him. And he appointed twelve, whom he also named apostles, to be with him, and to be sent out to proclaim the message, and to have authority to cast out demons" (Mark 3:13-15).

The same message that Jesus proclaimed was transferred to the lips of the apostles. Jesus declared the arrival of the kingdom of God in his person. Just so, the apostles announced from village to village that the future reign of God, which was to bring in the glorious age, had broken into this present darkness. The popular Jewish apocalyptic was that this age would be replaced with the age to come at the coming of the Messiah. The kingdom of God was envisioned in political terms. A political ruler like David would reestablish the glory days of Israel by liberating it from the Roman oppressor. Jesus instead pictured the reign of God as a spiritual invasion that would first liberate the hearts of people from the imprisonment of sin. A new, otherworldly order had come alongside and was supplanting the ruler of this age. The apostles were given authority to release people from demons as a sign that the kingdom of God was penetrating the darkness. The message of the kingdom was confirmed in power by the signs of the kingdom. Jesus was now extending himself into the lives of the Twelve, who were being prepared in Jesus' presence to carry on in his absence.

Jesus' strategy illustrates a principle that church leaders witness regularly: Our ministries' reach is directly proportional to the breadth of our leadership base. Only to the extent that we have grown self-initiating, reproducing, fully devoted disciples can new ministries touch the brokenness of people's lives. Therefore we see unmet needs because we have not intentionally grown champions to meet those needs. However, Jesus knew the human limitation of his incarnate state. As a solitary human being his reach was limited. His strategy was designed to touch the whole world through the multiplication of carefully trained disciples. On the eve of his date with the cross, he saw how much fruit his deliberate strategy of multiplication would bear. He said to his disciples, "Very truly, I tell you, the one who believes in me will also do the works that I do and, in fact, will do greater works than these, because I am going to the Father" (John 14:12). How can it be that someone could do greater works than the Son of God? The "greater works" were most likely a matter of quantity more than quality. By Jesus' multiplication of himself in the Twelve, they would geographically cover far greater territory than he ever did in his limited itinerant ministry. By the power of the indwelling Holy Spirit carrying them to the entire known world, the sheer volume of Jesus' ministry would expand exponentially. And so it has been.

By focusing on a few, Jesus was not displaying indifference to the multitudes. Instead, Jesus had a different vision for reaching the masses than our approach through mass gatherings. Jesus had enough vision to think small. Robert Coleman captured Jesus' methodology with the turn of a phrase: "Jesus' concern was not with programs to reach the multitudes, but with men the multitudes would follow."[12] After internalization, multiplication was the second strategic reason why Jesus focused on a few.

The Absence of Intentional Discipling

Jesus focused on a few because that was the way to grow people and ensure transference of his heart and vision to them. This kind of relationship, however, has been lacking in many of our lives.

Much of my passion for intentional discipling comes from not wanting others to experience what happened to me. It is true that our deepest convictions come from our life experience. As a fearful, emotionally burdened seventh grader, with only tentative connections to the church, I responded to the invitation to attend a weekend church camp. I heard exactly what I needed that weekend. The preacher on Saturday wrapped up his message with Jesus' words and summons, "Come to me, all you that are weary and are carrying heavy burdens, and I will give you rest" (Matthew 11:28).

When the invitation came to receive Christ, I wanted what Jesus had to offer—rest. Putting my trust in Christ opened the floodgates, for oceans of love seemed to roll over me. That evening our camp counselor asked if anyone had something to share from the day's events. After some awkward silence I timidly raised my hand and volunteered my encounter with the living Christ. I remember being handed a decision card, which I completed and returned to my counselor. I received only the barest of guidance about what I should do now that I had this life-altering connection to Christ. I made a valiant effort to read my Bible daily upon returning home, because, I suppose, someone said that might be a good thing.

In retrospect, I thought that I might hear from someone from the church, since I had turned in the decision card. I heard from no one. The silence was resounding. As a shy seventh grader, it never occurred to me to go to someone in the know and say, "Okay, now what? How do I go about growing in this newfound love in my life?" Instead, I drifted for years, grateful that I had a companion in Jesus that I didn't have before, but I had no idea of what to do next.

This should never be! I lost a number of years when my heart was ripe to be nurtured in this new faith. Yes, Jesus has been gracious to hold on to me in spite of the human failure and providentially brought people into my life in my latter high school and college years who would engage me in a discipleship process, but the church did not serve as a disciple-making body. If making disciples is the mission of the church, why are churches generally not prepared to provide the nurturing environment that grows self-initiating, reproducing, fully devoted followers of Jesus?

We could close the discipleship gap if we adopted Jesus' approach. By investing in a few over a three-year period, Jesus was able to encourage and guide his disciples to internalize his message and mission. I was fortunate during my college years to have someone like Don make up for what I had not received in my stumbling start with Christ. Don's open heart and his generosity with his time effected transference through close association. Don's passion for Christ infected this disciple, and multiplication took place. When Don graduated from seminary, the junior high ministry was suddenly without its leader, but it was not without leadership. Don had left himself behind in me and others. The church staff invited me to continue what Don had started. For two summers during my college years I led the junior high ministry with my college peers. Don had prepared us for his departure.

We now turn our focus from the strategic reasons for Jesus' investment in a few to the way he prepared the disciples to carry on his mission after he returned to the Father. Jesus brought his disciples through a process of growth to the intended outcome, which was to carry on his mission. They went from clueless to complete in three years. How did Jesus do that?

4

JESUS' PREPARATORY
EMPOWERMENT MODEL

In chapter three we examined two strategic reasons for Jesus' selection of the Twelve—internalization and multiplication. Jesus focused on a few because that was the only way to transplant his heart and mission into the lives of his key followers. Internalization cannot happen through a mass transference to an audience but must occur in an interpersonal environment. True multiplication or reproduction is possible only when disciples so internalize the mission that they are motivated to pass it on to others. Robert Coleman writes, "The best work is always done with a few. Better to give a year or so to one or two men who learn what it means to conquer for Christ than to spend a lifetime with a congregation just keeping the program going."[1]

Coleman's comment leads us to the focus of this chapter. How did Jesus go about shaping and training the Twelve to become fishers of people? Did Jesus open a school? Did he offer semester courses the disciples could enroll in? Was there the carrot of a diploma, a certificate of apostleship that gave them the credentials to be apostles of Jesus? Did he appoint himself as chancellor of Jesus University? Was there a curriculum that Jesus wanted his students to master?

As important as Jesus' teaching was, his *person* became the vehicle for the transmission of his life to his disciples. David Watson draws into sharp focus the centrality of the person of Jesus: "When Buddha was dying, his disciples asked how they could best remember him. He told them not to bother; it was his teaching, not his person, that counted.

With Jesus it was altogether different. Everything centers on *him*, his person. Discipleship means knowing *him*, loving *him*, believing in *him*, being committed to *him*."[2] The message was enfleshed and inseparable from who he was. "Jesus' leadership development of his under-shepherds was not so much a course or a curriculum as it was a shared life."[3]

Living on this side of Pentecost, it is easy to forget where Jesus had to begin with the Twelve. Who were these apostles Jesus selected to walk with him? What did Jesus have to work with? Were they made out of superior stuff that gave them the innate ability to accomplish extraordinary things? It is a sobering fact that Jesus selected ordinary, plain vanilla people who were no different from you or me. This is brought home in a humorous way by an apocryphal memorandum spoofing a common way people are screened for professional ministry today (see fig. 4.1).[4]

It has been broadly observed that the disciples were the rawest of raw material when Jesus first got a hold of them. "They were poor men of humble birth, low station, mean occupations, who had never felt the stimulating influence of a liberal education, or of social intercourse with persons of cultivated minds."[5] They were not the kind of people who would give instant credibility to Jesus' ministry. In our day, when people want to start a new enterprise, they seek to assure their future constituents by lining their letterhead with names that inspire confidence. It would hardly have been reassuring for the Palestinian investor in this new venture to read, "Peter and Andrew, James and John, fishermen; Matthew, tax collector; Simon, religious zealot." The Twelve, with the exception of Judas Iscariot, were hicks from the hill country of Galilee whose accents would show that they were "uneducated and ordinary men" (Acts 4:13).

Not only did they not have privileged birth, positions of power in the religious establishment or an education that would qualify them to be legal scholars, they came with all the foibles of their day. "At the time of their call they were exceedingly ignorant, narrow-minded, superstitious, full of Jewish prejudices, misconceptions, and animosities. They had much to unlearn of what was bad, as well as much to learn of what was good, and they were both slow to learn and unlearn."[6] The disciples were products of their time with all its limitations, as in any age. They had absorbed the common view that women were not worthy to be taught the Torah. In one

Memorandum

TO:
Jesus, Son of Joseph
Woodcrafter Carpenter Shop
Nazareth

FROM:
Jordan Management Consultants
Jerusalem

Dear Sir:
Thank you for submitting the resumes of the twelve men you have picked for management positions in your new organization. All of them have now taken our battery of tests; we have not only run the results through our computer but also arranged personal interviews for each of them with our psychologist and vocational aptitude consultant.

It is the staff opinion that most of your nominees are lacking in background, education and vocational aptitude for the type of enterprise you are undertaking. They do not have the team concept. We would recommend that you continue your search for persons of experience in managerial ability and proven capability.

Simon Peter is emotionally unstable and given to fits of temper. Andrew has absolutely no qualities of leadership. The two brothers, James and John, the sons of Zebedee, place personal interest above company loyalty. Thomas demonstrates a questioning attitude that would tend to undermine morale.

We feel that it is our duty to tell you that Matthew has been blacklisted by the Greater Jerusalem Better Business Bureau. James, the son of Alphaeus, and Thaddaeus definitely have radical leanings, and they both registered a high score on the manic-depressive scale.

One of the candidates, however, shows great potential. He is a man of ability and resourcefulness, meets people well, has a keen business mind and has contacts in high places. He is highly motivated, ambitious and responsible. We recommend Judas Iscariot as your controller and right-hand man. All of the other profiles are self-explanatory.

We wish you every success in your new venture.

Sincerely yours,
Jordan Management Consultants

Figure 4.1. Memo to Jesus

incident Jesus remained at Jacob's well in Samaria speaking to a questionable woman while the disciples went to a nearby village to purchase food. Upon their return the disciples "were astonished that he was speaking with a woman" (John 4:27). For the disciples, speaking to a woman was even more scandalous than speaking to a despised Samaritan. Then there were James and John, who drew the ire of their ten companions when they were caught trying to outmaneuver the others for positions of power when Jesus came into his kingdom. When Jesus called the Twelve, they were a reclamation project of the first order. Just like us.

Yet their association with Jesus over a three-year period served to transform this ragtag group into world beaters. After the descent of the promised Holy Spirit at Pentecost, a group of frightened, cowardly disciples was transformed into fearless megaphones for the resurrected Christ. Two of the disciples, Peter and John, were arrested by the religious leaders and told to cease telling people that Jesus was alive. Respectfully, Peter and John declined to succumb to this pressure, instead stating that "there is salvation in no one else, for there is no other name under heaven given among mortals by which we must be saved" (Acts 4:12). Then we find this reluctant commendation in the text regarding Peter and John: "Now when they saw the boldness of Peter and John and realized that they were uneducated and ordinary men, they were amazed and recognized them as companions of Jesus" (Acts 4:13).

This leads us back to the focus of this chapter. How did Jesus set about shaping the Twelve into people prepared to carry on his work after he returned to the Father? Acts 4:13 echoes Mark's version of the call of the Twelve to be apostles: "And he appointed twelve, whom he also named apostles, to be with him" (Mark 3:14). Being *with* Jesus in a relational setting served as the basis to shape the disciples' character and instill Jesus' mission in them.

What relational, developmental process did Jesus take these disciples through so they would be ready to carry on his mission? At the outset we must acknowledge that there is no clear, step-by-step formula outlined in the Gospels. Attempts have been made to fit the gospel content into distinct phases, as if Jesus were operating out of a sequential leadership-development model. Though I will describe a developmental process through which the disciples progressed, the stages were overlapping and repetitive. Human beings grow, fall back, relearn, stumble forward, lose their way, get back on track. Our growth process is somewhat like a sine wave on a gradual uphill course, taking a person in zigzag fashion to a higher level. It is often only in retrospect that we realize progress is being made. Martin Luther King Jr. used to close many of his talks with the old slave's prayer: "O God, I ain't what I ought to be and I ain't what I'm gonna be, but thanks be to you, I ain't what I used to be."[7]

Pre-Disciple (Inquiry) Stage

Before I outline the developmental stages Jesus brought the disciples through, it is important to acknowledge that a hard line must be crossed to enter into this growth process. There is no formation without submission. In the pre-disciple phase, described as stage one in chapter three (see pages 63-64), the disciples control the inquiry. We noted in John 1 that Andrew and the "other" disciple tag along after Jesus when he comes on the scene. Jesus says to them, "What are you looking for?" (John 1:38). The two indicate that they want some time with Jesus in order to satisfy themselves that he is the promised One. Jesus says simply, "Come and see" (John 1:39). They are the investigators, and Jesus is the subject.

But in order for discipleship to occur, the tables must be turned. The seeking ones must become the submitted ones. The bold line between "come and see" and "come and follow me" must be crossed. Only then does Jesus exercise his shaping influence over their lives. This is where Jesus pulls the great reversal on the accepted way that disciples attached themselves to a rabbi. The standard practice was that disciples investigated various rabbis and decided who they wanted to follow. In other words, the disciples controlled their destinies. Not so with Jesus. Michael Wilkins observes, "Whereas discipleship was a voluntary initiative with other types of master-disciple relationships in the first century, with Jesus the initiative lay with his choice and call of those who would be his disciples."[8] Up to this point, Andrew (and John) were like any other disciples seeking a rabbi. Soon the tables would be turned, and Jesus would issue the call, "Come and follow me," which required a yes or no. This concept is integral to the nature of discipleship. Jesus must be in the lead position and on his terms.

Once this line had been crossed, Jesus led the disciples through a four-stage preparatory process (see table 4.1). Two insights from a popular leadership model helped open my eyes to Jesus' growth process with the disciples. Paul Hersey and Ken Blanchard, in *Situational Leadership*, state that good leaders do two things. First, they have a readiness goal in mind for their followers. Second, they adjust their leadership style to the level of preparedness of an individual or group in order to progress toward the readiness goal. Hersey and Blanchard define readiness as "the ability and willingness of a person or group to take responsibility for directing their own behavior."[9] Their theory is that there is no one best or right style of leadership, but a leader's style must be adapted to fit the readiness level of those he or she is helping to reach the goal.

Table 4.1. Jesus' preparatory empowerment process

	PRE-DISCIPLE	STAGE 1	STAGE 2	STAGE 3	STAGE 4
Jesus' role	The inviter	The living example	The provocative teacher	The supportive coach	The ultimate delegator
The disciples' role	Seekers	Observers and imitators	Students and questioners	Short-term missionaries	Apostles
Readiness level	Hungry to know whether Jesus was the long-awaited Messiah	Ready to observe who Jesus is and the nature of his ministry and mission	Ready to interact with Jesus and publicly identify with him	Ready to test the authority of Jesus to work through them	Ready to assume full responsibility for making reproducing disciples
Key questions	Is Jesus the Messiah?	Who is Jesus, and what is his ministry and mission?	What is the cost of following Jesus?	Will the power of Jesus work through us when we take on his ministry?	Will I give my life entirely to the mission of making reproducing disciples?

In the same way, Jesus called his disciples "to be with him" with the readiness goal of carrying on in his absence. "He knew what they could not yet see, that He had chosen them in order to train them as the future leaders in the church and mission field, for the day that He would leave them."[10] Jesus had a clear goal to be reached in three years. In chapter three we reflected on George Martin's three-year challenge: what difference would it make in the way we, as leaders, spent our time if we knew that we had only three years remaining in our current ministry and there would be no leaders to replace us? Jesus lived with this sense of destiny. He was on a short timetable and had to bring his replacements to a state of readiness. What was Jesus' readiness goal? It was that the disciples would assume full responsibility for being and making self-initiating, reproducing, fully devoted followers. But to do that he had to begin where they were and carefully shape them through a preparatory development process. What was that process?

Jesus acted as a master trainer. His life destiny was the cross. He was the man born to die. Yet converging on that moment would be the necessity of having his disciples prepared to carry on his mission after his resurrection and return to the Father. To get the disciples ready, Jesus played a series of important roles, commensurate with the disciples' preparedness. At stage one, early in his ministry, Jesus was a *living example*. The disciples watched him carefully and therefore began to absorb his message, manner and ministry. At stage two, Jesus was a *provocative teacher*. Jesus' intent was not only to inform the disciples of a new kingdom perspective but also to dislodge the wrong-headed ideas and assumptions they had picked up from a religious and secular world in rebellion against God. At stage three, Jesus was a *supportive coach*. The disciples were sent on a short-term mission within Jesus' clear instructions, knowing that he was there for a supportive debriefing on their return. At stage four, Jesus was the *ultimate delegator*. The disciples had internalized enough to survive their scattering at Jesus' crucifixion, and to be regrouped after the resurrection and empowered by the Holy Spirit at Pentecost. His ministry had become theirs.

Developmental Stage One: Jesus, the Living Example

At this first stage of their development, the disciples needed to comprehend the nature of Jesus' ministry and mission, and to ask the all-important question: Who is this person who says and does such phenomenal things? In the initial stages of training, the leader needs to be highly directive. The leader sets the agenda and defines the roles of the neophytes. For Jesus this meant that he presented himself as the living example for the disciples to observe and study. "Knowledge was gained by association before it was understood by explanation."[11] "I do; you watch" describes this stage.

It appears that early in Jesus' ministry the role of disciples was to be quiet observers. The disciples are present at the various encounters or teachings of Jesus, but they remain in the background. One has the sense that they are standing off to the side, observing Jesus in action. He is the focus. "This was the essence of his training program—just letting his disciples follow him."[12] Jesus' approach was similar to the role of a rabbi in the life of a student. In the rabbinic model a disciple literally copied a life. Rabbis were considered to be the living Torah—the rule of life with skin on. Referring to the rabbinical approach, Birger Gerhardsson writes,

> To learn one must go to a Teacher. . . . But they also learn a great deal by simply observing: with attentive eyes they observe all that the teacher does and then proceed to imitate him. Torah is above all a holy, authoritative attitude towards life and way of life. Because this is true, much can be learned simply by watching and imitating those who are learned.[13]

Let's look at one portion of the Gospels from the standpoint of the disciples' role. In the first five chapters of the Gospel of Mark, the disciples are mentioned only sporadically—just enough to let us know that they are present. Mark emphasizes three things about Jesus that the disciples observe. First, Mark focuses on Jesus' *authority* over the demoniac (Mark 1:21-28; 5:1-20), over sin (Mark 2:1-12), over the sabbath (Mark 2:23–3:6), over nature (Mark 4:35-41), over illness and disease (Mark 1:40-45; 5:21-34) and even over death (Mark 5:35-43).

Second, Mark paints a picture of the kinds of people Jesus' heart went out to: the demoniacs (Mark 1:23; 5:2), the leper (Mark 1:40), the paralyzed man (Mark 2:3), Levi the tax collector (Mark 2:14), a man with a withered hand (Mark 3:1), a hemorrhaging woman (Mark 5:25), and a ruler of the synagogue and his daughter close to death (Mark 5:35-42).

Third, Mark dramatizes the religious establishment's antagonism toward Jesus. The Pharisees mock Jesus' authority to forgive the paralytic

(Mark 2:6-7), disdain his eating with tax collectors and sinners (Mark 2:16), are shocked that he and his disciples apparently violate the sabbath (Mark 2:24), watch in wait for him to heal on the sabbath (Mark 3:2), and declare that Jesus is demon possessed (Mark 3:22).

As Jesus establishes his authority over the forces of evil, demonstrates his heart for the outcast and receives the antagonism of the religious establishment, the disciples are essentially taking it all in. What appearances do the disciples make in the first five chapters of Mark? Beyond the four fishermen responding to the call to follow Jesus, the disciples appear in the form of "they" when Jesus enters the synagogue in Capernaum and delivers a man with an unclean spirit (Mark 1:21-28) and at the home of Andrew and Peter, where Jesus heals Peter's mother-in-law (Mark 1:29-31). Peter and the others next appear in their frantic search for Jesus, who has slipped away to a "deserted place" to be with his Father (Mark 1:35-39). Otherwise they receive only brief mention. They are dinner guests in the home of Levi, the tax collector (Mark 2:15-17). They become an issue because they are not fasting, while John the Baptist's and the Pharisees' disciples fast (Mark 2:18). They are a source of controversy since they plucked heads of grain from the fields on the sabbath (Mark 2:23-28). In Mark 3 there is the definitive moment when Jesus chooses the twelve who were to be his apostles (Mark 3:13-15). Yet Jesus seems to be in no particular hurry at this time for them to enter into this mission, since there is a considerable delay between their designation as apostles and their being sent out by Jesus. In Mark 4 the disciples' fear is aroused by the storm that threatens their lives and is replaced by an even greater fear once Jesus commands the storm to cease. The disciples' last appearance in the first five chapters of Mark is Peter, James and John's presence when Jesus raises Jairus's daughter.

The disciples' only substantive interaction with Jesus in the first five chapters of Mark occurs after Jesus' public teaching on the parable of the soils. Otherwise the disciples tag along. But they are not nonentities. The telling question occurs after Jesus' stilling of the storm, when the disciples ask, "Who then is this, that even the wind and the sea obey him?" (Mark 4:41). In the observe-imitate stage, these questions predominate:

Who is this man? Who does he think he is? Fascination with the person of Jesus forms the basis for discipleship.

Even though this may be the foundational stage of discipleship, observation-imitation continues as a means of formation throughout Jesus' ministry. Just prior to his crucifixion Jesus kneels before each of them to wash their feet, just as a household servant would do for an invited guest. Even here at the end of Jesus' earthly ministry, the disciples still have not grasped that greatness is measured by descent, not ascent. Jesus has to go beyond verbal instruction to modeling. After washing the feet of each of the disciples, he draws the incident to a close by making explicit the point of his action: "If I, your Lord and Teacher, have washed your feet, you also ought to wash one another's feet. For I have set you an example, that you also should do as I have done to you" (John 13:14-15).

Jesus stated this principle explicitly when he said, "A disciple is not above the teacher, but everyone who is fully qualified will be like the teacher" (Luke 6:40). At the most basic level a disciple is simply a learner. The first level of learning is the desire to be like a model. Jesus is saying that discipleship training is not about information transfer, from head to head, but imitation, life to life.

My wife was an elementary school principal. Prior to her career as a principal she earned her spurs by teaching at almost every elementary school grade level. Over her career, which spanned almost three decades, she had witnessed numerous advances in educational theory and technology. The classroom had become a much more stimulating place. There was no need for a child to be bored, for there were many ways to learn. Yet she constantly reminds me that one thing has not changed and never will change: the people factor. The most important ingredient in motivating a child to learn is the bond between the teacher and the student. The old expression is still quite true: "People don't care how much you know until they know how much you care."

The magnetic attraction of the life and ministry of Jesus became the focus of the disciples in this initial stage.

Developmental Stage Two: Jesus, the Provocative Teacher

It is fascinating to watch Jesus' leadership style vary in relationship to the readiness of his followers. Jesus, though, was not just responding to the disciples' readiness level. Jesus intentionally changed his leadership style in order to provoke the apostles to a new stage of readiness as well. At this second stage Jesus acts as a *provocative teacher*. Jesus instructs or questions his apostles apart from the crowds in order to confound them and cause them to rethink their basic worldview. Jesus continues to lead in these moments, but he draws the disciples into interaction so that they can assess what it will take to be a follower of Jesus. This stage is summed up by "I do; you help."

Jesus taught his disciples in the live encounters in the midst of ministry. Class was always in session. As Jesus taught, preached and healed, he was conscious that these settings served as training events for the few. First the disciples heard or observed Jesus in his public ministry, and then with regularity Jesus turned to them to offer further explanation or pose questions.

Let's examine two instructive moments when Jesus turned from either teaching the crowds or engaging in dialogue in order to interact with his disciples. Just as a would-be disciple today begins a relationship with Jesus with a host of half-truths, misguided thoughts and lies, so did the Twelve. These interactions are intended to unmask and confront those attitudes and values that are not in line with Jesus' kingdom perspective. For the disciples these were gut-check times; they had to assess the cost and commitment necessary to identify with Jesus. They had their cherished assumptions and worldviews challenged.

The first incident, found in Mark 7, records Jesus' confrontation with the scribes and Pharisees over a difference of opinion about the nature of righteousness. To the religious leaders, righteousness was equated with outward behavior, such as ritual washing of hands prior to touching food. To Jesus, righteousness was first and foremost a matter of heart. Jesus summarized his position, "Then he called the crowd again and said to them, 'Listen to me, all of you, and understand: there is nothing outside a person that by going in can defile, but the things that come out are what defile'" (Mark 7:14-15). At this point Jesus makes a deliberate shift from the public to a private moment: "When he had left the crowd and entered the house, his disciples asked him about the parable" (Mark 7:17). Jesus drives home his point with pressing questions: "Then do you also fail to understand? Do you not see that whatever goes into a person from outside cannot defile, since it enters, not the heart but the stomach, and goes out into the sewer?" (Mark 7:18-19). The disciples were slow to get Jesus' point, because they had a view of righteousness more akin to that of the religious leaders, since their teaching predominated. Only in these private moments could Jesus reframe their understanding of truth.

A second encounter, in Mark 10, becomes another occasion in which Jesus corrects the theological myths that the disciples have absorbed. A man we have come to know as the "rich young ruler" approaches Jesus. Here is a great catch, if he can be reeled in. The young man seems eager enough. "Good Teacher, what must I do to inherit eternal life?" (Mark 10:17). Jesus responds with a mysterious retort, "Why do you call me good?"[14] In response to what he must do, Jesus enumerates some of the Ten Commandments. On hearing these the rich young ruler pronounces himself spotless. But Jesus doesn't accept his self-justification. He exposes his god: "You lack one thing; go, sell what you own . . . then come, follow me" (Mark 10:21). Jesus calls the question. The young ruler walks away grieving because of his attachment to his great wealth.

Immediately Jesus swivels toward the disciples and draws the conclusion, "How hard it will be for those who have wealth to enter the kingdom of God!" (Mark 10:23). Mark records the reaction of the disciples. They are perplexed. All of their lives they have been taught that there is an inseparable positive correlation between wealth and righteousness. If you are wealthy, God must have blessed you. Picking up on their befuddlement, Jesus drives a deeper wedge between righteousness and wealth with a graphic image: "It is easier for a camel to go through the eye of a needle than for someone who is rich to enter the kingdom of God." Now the disciples are exasperated: "Then who can be saved?" (Mark 10:25-26).

Jesus allowed the disciples to live with conundrums. He intentionally set up mental train wrecks. Running on the same tracks toward each other were two diametrically opposed thoughts. No easy answers were provided, nor were there fill-in-the-blank workbooks. He wanted disciples who would have to think through the issues. Included in discipleship is the discipleship of the mind. Too much of the material that is produced under the heading of discipleship curriculum is spoon-fed pabulum. Jesus intentionally troubled the disciples by challenging their cherished assumptions.

In a discipling relationship, life circumstance becomes the setting for the exegetical work of God's Word. My discipling relationships over the years have offered no end of opportunities to reflect on the Word of God in teachable moments. One of my discipling partners was in the midst of an interminable lawsuit over a dream house that had burned down during the latter stages of construction. Mike's first Sunday at our church was the Sunday following this upsetting experience. It "just so happened" that the Scripture and subject of that Sunday morning's message was Yahweh speaking to Moses via the burning bush. Mike immediately understood that the ashes of his home were his burning bush. Yet the event that grabbed his attention and brought him to the Lord continued to be the source of much further instruction through years of litigation. Our Americanized version of God's blessing assumes an ever-increasing financial position. Mike's financial position became ever decreasing following his coming to Christ. How do we understand God's blessing in these circumstances? We discussed how the American view of blessing had overshadowed Jesus' view.

The most crucial and climactic interactive dialogue between Jesus and the disciples centered on the personal question that every potential disciple of Jesus must answer. Jesus asked the disciples two questions that moved from the general to the specific. His first question was a setup: "Who do people say that I am?" (Mark 8:27). The disciples relayed the scuttlebutt they had heard on the road. Then Jesus turned to them with *the* question, "But who do you say that I am?" (Mark 8:29). After Peter miraculously blurted out the right answer, "You are the Messiah," Jesus went on to fill out the conception of Messiah as a suffering servant, terms that were diametrically opposed to the popular conception. A dying messiah was unthinkable to Peter. In the space of a few moments Peter went from being an instrument of God's revelation to an unwitting tool of Satan. Peter rebuked Jesus for articulating the ridiculous idea that he would set his face to go to Jerusalem and die at the hands of the unrighteous. The notion of choosing to lay down one's life became the occasion for Jesus to explain the cost of discipleship for any who would follow him.

In addition to these interactive teaching moments, Jesus affirmed the disciples' value by including them as his assistants. On one occasion Jesus attempted to get away to a quiet place in order to debrief their mission. The crowds would not allow Jesus out of their sight, so they followed him and the Twelve to a deserted place. Being far from a nearby town where the people could obtain food, the disciples became concerned that the crowd had nothing to eat. Initially, Jesus placed the responsibility on the disciples to feed the five thousand. The disciples checked their treasury and determined that two hundred denarii would not go very far. At this point Jesus took over. He miraculously multiplied five loaves and two fish into enough food to feed everyone. The disciples were prominent as Jesus' ushers at this outdoor gathering. They divided the crowd into groups of hundreds and fifties, and distributed the bread and fish in an orderly fashion. The disciples in this instance were extensions of the ministry of Jesus to the people. The disciples were visible and prominent, even as Jesus continued to be the one the crowds looked to.

There is a great training principle here. If we are to follow the model of Jesus, apprenticeship should be a part of all we do so that ministry can be multiplied. Small-group leaders identify apprentices with the potential to lead. They are given increasing responsibility from week to week so that it is obvious to the other group members those being groomed for future leadership. A pastor should never visit the hospital or go on a grief call alone, seeing it as the opportunity to train those called to caring ministry. When I was attempting to expand a seminar to help God's people discern their spiritual gifts and call to ministry, I rewrote the curriculum and taught it with two other lay leaders with teaching gifts. They put their fingerprints on the curriculum and their teaching style on the workshop. What we created and delivered together was by far better than anything I could have done on my own. When speaking opportunities arise, especially to teach in the areas of discipling or missions, I invite those with whom I have been in a discipling relationship so they can add their word of witness but also hear from me again the vision connected with these emphases.

A number of benefits accrue when assistants are publicly included in ministry. First, those assisting gain a sense of their value to the one who has included them. For the disciples, I am sure they began to realize their importance and value by their public association with Jesus. Second, the public identification with a leader deepens their ownership of the mission. The mission of Jesus slowly became the disciples' mission through visibility. Third, apprenticeship heightens the learning curve. When people are being trained to lead a future mission, their learning antenna is wired to observe more carefully and to seek answers to questions that will equip them when they are in a position of responsibility.

In this second stage, where Jesus acted as the provocative teacher, he raised the bar for the disciples through his personalized instruction, pointed questioning and lifting their public profile.

Developmental Stage Three: Jesus, the Supportive Coach

In the third phase of Jesus' preparatory model, Jesus acts as the *supportive coach* by sending the Twelve and the Seventy out on a short-term mission opportunity. From the time Jesus designated the Twelve to be apostles, he had this moment in mind. Their mission had been clearly defined. They were to be "sent out to proclaim the message, and to have authority to cast out demons" (Mark 3:14-15). Yet there was a time delay between Jesus' stated destination and the Twelve assuming this responsibility. Jesus wanted them to slowly live into this role. This stage is marked by "You do; I help."

Jesus intentionally adjusts his leadership style again in order to move the disciples to a new stage of development. Jesus acts as the coach sending them on their mission, and yet he remains supportive, ready to debrief them on their return. Jesus sends out the Twelve and the Seventy into the fray with the knowledge that he will be there on their return to cheer their successes and address their quandaries. While an apprentice probably never feels fully ready to assume the lead role, like baby birds Jesus' disciples needed to be pushed out of the nest to see if they were going to fly. They also knew that the nest was still there for them to return to after their initial flight.

Jesus was a model delegator. Once Jesus completed his instructions, the disciples not only knew their mission but also had specific guidelines to follow in order to accomplish it.

Matthew gives us the most detailed account of the mission Jesus sends the Twelve on: clear instructions, clear authority and clear expectations.

Clear instructions. Matthew introduces the mission with this line: "These twelve Jesus sent out with the following instructions" (Matthew 10:5). I often hear pastors say that they delegate ministry to members of their congregation, meaning that they have dumped a responsibility in the lap of a willing recipient without any clarity of mission or guidelines about how to carry it out. Not so with Jesus. Note the specificity of Jesus' instructions (Matthew 10:5-15). The *parameters* of the mission were that they went only to the lost sheep of Israel, and not to the Gentiles. The *focus* of the mission was proclaiming the message of the kingdom. The *demonstration* of the mission was to cure the sick, raise the dead, cleanse the lepers and cast out demons. The *means* to accomplish the mission was that they were not to rely on any earthly means of support. They were to stay with those who received the message. The *response* to the mission was that if people did not welcome them, they were to walk away and leave the judgment to God.

Clear authority. To be effective, authority must be delegated along with responsibility to accomplish a mission. Yet in the church, people often feel that they have been given a responsibility without authority. Each decision must be approved by a higher up because people have not been entrusted with the capacity to implement the direction they discern. Jesus gave the disciples the parameters in which to function and then gave them his full backing to accomplish what he gave them to do.

Clear expectations. After detailing the clear instructions and authority, Jesus also warned the disciples about what lay ahead (Matthew 10:16-42). He wove together the cost and privilege of discipleship. If popularity with the world was the disciples' hoped-for outcome, then they had the wrong cause. They would face a rough crowd. Jesus compared the world to a pack of wolves. Awaiting them would be floggings by the authorities and betrayal by family members. After all, if this is what happened to their master, how much more could the servants expect the same? And yet there is great privilege in representing the name of Jesus and bearing his fate. "Everyone therefore who acknowledges me before others, I also will acknowledge before my Father in heaven," Jesus says (Matthew 10:32). Just as a coach exhorts his players before a football game, "Leave it all on the field," so Jesus is saying, "Pay the necessary price, because you will have my approval."

The Twelve and the Seventy engaged in this short-term mission project with the full knowledge that Jesus would be there for the debriefing on their return. In a sense this was an experimental, limited foray that served as a precursor to the life mission that was ahead after Jesus returned to the Father. The Gospels convey a sense of excitement and questioning when the Twelve and the Seventy reported back to Jesus. Mark captures their enthusiasm in this way: "The apostles gathered around Jesus, and told him all that they had done and taught" (Mark 6:30). Luke reports that the Seventy "returned with joy" (Luke 10:17). Yet there were cases that appeared to be beyond their resources, and these demanded further instruction from Jesus.

What were the benefits for the disciples from the short-term mission? First, they gained confidence in the authority of Jesus. Just as Jesus promised, people were healed, demons were cast out and the good news of the gospel was received. Jesus truly had given them his authority to carry out the mission! Second, they grew in competence. Ultimately, you can learn and develop only by doing. Toward the end of my first professional ministry with college students, one of our student leaders gave me what I took to be a backhanded compliment: "You have really grown as a teacher." I should have said, "Thank you," and left it at that. But my reply caused her to say, "When you first began teaching, you weren't very good." Ouch! But it was true. Only through the students' patience and forbearance did my teaching gift emerge. Just so, the disciples needed a controlled laboratory in which to practice.

But third, the disciples also faced their shortcomings. When we get in over our heads, beyond our confidence and competence, we become open to learning. An exasperated father approached Jesus because his disciples could not cast out a demon that tormented his son. Jesus proceeded with considerable impatience to do what the disciples could not. Later the disciples took advantage of the private moment to ask Jesus, "Why could we not cast it out?" (Mark 9:28). Jesus says, essentially, that this kind of an entrenched demonic spirit requires another level of prayer and fasting.

Delegation is a necessary stage to faith and leadership development. When a child learns to ride a bike, at some point the training wheels have to come off. The maiden voyage is a combination of terror and thrill. We make our way in wobbly fashion down the sidewalk and hope our crash is softened by the neighbor's lawn. We pick ourselves up and get back on the bike and try again and again. Eventually, riding a bike becomes an internalized behavior so that no matter how long the time gaps between rides, we know how to keep our balance. Growth in serving Jesus is always like that. We must go where we have never gone before, with all the terror and thrill that comes with new territory. We find that Jesus is there to support and do through us just what he said he would. Jesus is never more pleased than when we trust him.

Developmental Stage Four: Jesus, the Ultimate Delegator

Jesus staked his entire ministry on the preparation of the Twelve to carry on his mission after he returned to the Father. The time had come to send the disciples on their own mission of reproduction. Jesus acts as the *ultimate delegator.* Jesus had a divine appointment with the cross, which the Scripture refers to as "the hour" (Mark 14:41; John 4:21; 12:23; 16:25; 17:1) or "his hour" (John 7:30; 8:20; 13:1). "The hour has come" converges with the transference of Jesus' ministry to the Twelve. Jesus' mission is complete in his death and resurrection. And at this time Jesus makes it clear that the focus of his work has been preparing the disciples to assume their leadership role under the guidance of his Spirit, not his physical presence. "You do; I watch" sums up this stage.

Jesus' pre-crucifixion ministry concludes by his huddling with the Twelve around the Passover meal (John 13–17). The foundational importance of the Twelve to his ongoing mission is demonstrated by sharing his last hours alone with them. We come to a most sacred moment. We are allowed to eavesdrop on Jesus' final prayer before his rendezvous with death. What was on Jesus' heart? Two things: he anticipated a reunion with his Father, and he prayed for the Twelve.

Jesus is fully conscious that he is completing what the Father had sent him to do. "I glorified you on earth by finishing the work that you gave me to do" (John 17:4). He nostalgically longs to return to his privileged position of a face-to-face relationship with the Father, which had been true prior to the creation of the world. Jesus is homesick. "So now, Father, glorify me in your own presence with the glory that I had in your presence before the world existed" (John 17:5). Jesus recalls life at home in the heart of the Father. He can't wait to salve the ache of separation that will be complete in face-to-face communion.

Though this prayer is wrapped in an atmosphere of Jesus' longing to be at home, the center of the prayer focuses solely on the Twelve. Jesus says that he doesn't even pray on behalf of the lost and rebellious world, but for those the Father has given him out of the world (John 17:9). The final preparation of the Twelve was a significant part of finishing his work. His work would not have been completed until the Twelve were ready to assume their foreordained position. The tragedy is that most Christian leaders have placed almost no priority on transitional leadership. It is generally fair to say that the effectiveness of one's ministry is to be measured by how well it flourishes after one's departure.

For what does Jesus pray for his disciples? He prays for their protection and that they may be one; that they would be kept from the evil one; that they would not fall into apostasy, as did Judas; that Jesus' joy would be complete in them; that they would be made holy in the truth of God's Word (John 17:11-16). Then he makes the transitional mission statement, "As you have sent me into the world, so I have sent them into the world" (John 17:18). His ministry has now become their ministry. Not only are they sent but they are also to reproduce. Jesus prays not only for these Twelve but also for those who would believe because of their witness (John 17:20). Earlier in this Passover gathering, Jesus said, "My Father is glorified by this, that you bear much fruit and become my disciples" (John 15:8). In John's typical fashion, the nature of the fruit bearing is deliciously ambiguous. We should take this quantitatively (that more disciples are made) and qualitatively (that the disciples would reflect the character and life of Jesus). As Dawson Trotman said, the apostles are "born to reproduce," which can be said of every disciple of Jesus.

Here is the challenge to all pastors and Christian leaders. Where are the men and women in whom we are multiplying ourselves so that the ministry carries on long after we have gone? How would your ministry be different if you placed the highest priority on selecting, motivating and training lay leaders who could carry on, as much as possible, the mission of the parish after you were gone? Take a moment to evaluate how your ministry would be different if you made a few the priority, as Jesus did. What if you adopted Jesus' model of training a few by guiding them through all these developmental stages to the point where their ministry did not rely on you? How would the way you spend your time change? How would this affect your weekly schedule? What would you have to give up doing in order to train people? What skills would you have to acquire that are not currently a part of your repertoire? Robert Coleman writes, "What really counts in the ultimate perpetuation of our work is the faithfulness with which our converts go out and make leaders out of their converts, not simply more followers."[15]

Jesus employed an empowerment model of servant leadership and training. Whereas pastors and ministry leaders today tend to be satisfied in having people become dependent on their teaching and care, Jesus wanted self-initiating, reproducing, fully devoted followers. Today's pastor often looks at the church as the context in which he or she can minister while gathering a congregation as the audience. Jesus, by contrast, thought that multiplication of ministry in a chosen few was the measurement of success. I am sorry to say that what Coleman prophetically wrote in 1963 is still largely true: "Jesus' plan has not been disavowed; it has been ignored."[16] If we want to see the mark of our ministry be self-initiating, reproducing, fully devoted followers, we must adopt Jesus' method of investing in a few as the foundation on which to build our ministry.

In chapter five we will see that the apostle Paul had an empowerment model similar to Jesus', though he used different images to convey the same reality.

5

Paul's Empowerment Model

Spiritual Parenting

In chapter four we examined Jesus' preparatory disciple-making model with insights from *Situational Leadership*. My thesis is that Jesus adapted his leadership style to the readiness level of the disciples. His goal was to equip the Twelve to continue his mission. From the beginning the incarnate Son of God intended to extend his life and ministry through this small core of disciples by setting up an interlocking, multigenerational chain of disciple making (John 17:20).

We turn our attention now to the apostle Paul's model of disciple making. We must first note that the language running throughout the Gospels and the book of Acts is absent in Paul's writings. Whereas the terms *make disciples* and *be a disciple* dominate Jesus' vocabulary and the historical account of the early church in Acts, they are nowhere to be found in Paul's letters. In fact, Paul never speaks of having disciples![1] Paul shifts away from discipleship terminology to what we have come to call "spiritual formation" language, because of the post-Pentecost focus on the indwelling presence of the Holy Spirit. His efforts were directed toward helping the church understand that Christians are "in Christ" and vice versa (Christ in you). This does not mean that the concept of discipleship is absent in Paul's thought. Being a self-initiating, reproducing, fully devoted follower of Christ is as much present in Paul's thought as it is in Jesus' thought. It is just stated in *spiritual formation* terms.[2]

The defining, though not exclusive, metaphor that shapes Paul's understanding of the goal and the process of disciple making is spiritual parenting.

Paul's writings are sprinkled with images of spiritual fatherhood and motherhood: addressing those under his care as infants and children; characterizing himself as a nursing mother or as a mother in the agony of labor, or as a father with his children, stating that the goal in Christ is to grow up to maturity (adulthood). Though Paul does not restrict himself to this group of family images, the lens that shapes the primary way he views the process and product of being in Christ is parental.

The Goal of Parenting

In a healthy family the goal of parents is to grow children into independent, responsible and caring adults who live independently. Jack and Judy Balswick provide an excellent overview of family images in the growth process.

> The Christian life is described in various New Testament passages as growth from spiritual infancy to maturity. The new believer starts as an infant and eventually grows up in Christ. One moves from a state of dependency, in which others model, teach, and disciple, to a mature walk with God. As this growth occurs, the believer also begins to assume discipling responsibility for others. While it is true that the believer is always dependent on God and the Holy Spirit in that growth process, there is a natural progression in maturity which leads the believer to be used by God to serve and minister to others.[3]

The Balswicks quite naturally weave together a biblical conception of parenting with the parental images for the Christian growth process. "Parenting which empowers children to maturity is conceptually similar to the New Testament depiction of discipling."[4] The way the Balswicks conceive of the goal of Christian parenting sounds much like a definition of Christian maturity. "Successful parenting will result in the children's gaining as much personal power as the parents themselves have. In the Christian context, children who have been empowered love God and their neighbors as themselves. They are capable of going beyond themselves to reach out to others."[5]

It should not surprise us that the goal of Christian parenting is identical to the goal of discipling. The primary discipleship unit is the Christian home. The primary disciplers are parents. That Paul should weave parental and developmental images into his understanding of the maturity process makes all the sense in the world.

Paul's Empowerment Goal

For Paul the primary goal of the Christian life is to reach the state of maturity in Christ. Paul personalized Jesus' clarion call to "make disciples" in writing his own mission statement. Paul simply takes Jesus' mission for the church and states it in his own words. "It is he [Jesus] whom we proclaim, warning everyone and teaching everyone in all wisdom, so that we may present everyone mature in Christ. For this I toil and struggle with all the energy that he powerfully inspires within me" (Colossians 1:28-29). A singular mission demands all of Paul's effort and energy—to bring everyone to maturity in Christ.

We can detect the call of God on a person's life by listening for what energizes them. Paul doesn't make us guess the mission that has captured his heart, because he tells us directly what energizes him, using the word *energy* twice in verse 29. He speaks of the "energy which *powerfully inspires* [literally *energizes*] *him*." One of the synonyms that Paul uses for spiritual gifts occurs in 1 Corinthians 12:6, "There are different kinds of working [literally *energizings*]" (NIV). When we operate in accord with our spiritual gifts in the context of our call, we have plugged into divine energy. Therefore Paul puts all of his effort into bringing people to adulthood in Christ.

Paul begins Colossians 1:29 with "For this I toil." The root of the Greek word for "toil" means beatings or the weariness that comes from being struck. As this term evolved, it became an analogy for the weariness that comes from hard work, labor or striving. This image is coupled with "struggle." "For this I toil and struggle." A literal transliteration from the Greek would be "agonize."[6] On another occasion Paul used this same word to compare the Christian life with that of an athlete: "Athletes exercise [agonize] self-control in all things; they do it to receive a perishable wreath, but we an imperishable one" (1 Corinthians 9:25). Paul is plugged into God's power through the knowledge that he is doing what God designed and chose him to do.

Paul's goal for everyone is "maturity in Christ." In fact, the root of the word for "maturity" in Greek is *telos*, which means "end" or "goal." To be mature is to be fully adult. J. B. Lightfoot believes that Paul has intentionally imported this word from the ancient mystery religions. According to the mystery religions, the fully instructed were the mature, as opposed to novices. In the early church the baptized were the *teleios* ("mature" or "complete"), as opposed to the catechumens, who were still in a preparatory or instructional period prior to baptism. To further underscore the family connections with this word, Paul contrasts being mature with being infants or children in the faith. Paul chides the Corinthians "as infants in Christ," who are still drinking milk when they should be eating solid food (1 Corinthians 3:1-2). Later in this same letter Paul draws a direct contrast between being children versus being adults: "Brothers and sisters, do not be children in your thinking; rather ... in thinking be adults [*teleios*]" (1 Corinthians 14:20). In Ephesians Paul states that the mature (*teleios*) have grown to the measure of full stature of Christ, whereas those who are children in the faith are unstable, tossed around and carried away by the wind of every new doctrine that is enticing (Ephesians 4:13-14).

Yet Paul's goal of maturity for all believers must be coupled with a process of transformation that gets us there.

Transformation: Product and Process

Essentially, Scripture says each one of us is a reclamation project. God is in the salvage business. We are in need of transformation or a makeover. As I was growing up, I watched a dramatic transformation take place. Scholl Canyon in Southern California was a gorge where the trash trucks unloaded their rotting garbage and human discards. Yet in my twenties I had the opportunity to play golf on this same site. It had been *transformed* from a stinking landfill to a beautifully manicured, green playground overlooking the San Fernando Valley. Once the ravine was filled to capacity, it was *changed* from a refuse depository into a new creation or a place of recreation.

Paul uses a couple of images that describe the transformation or makeover that is to be a continuous lifestyle of apprentices of Christ. *Makeover* is an appropriate term because Paul speaks of undressing and redressing. First, we are to put off the old, tattered, soiled garments that represent our former life apart from Christ. In Ephesians 4:22 Paul says, "You were taught to put away your former way of life, your old self." Undress. In its place we are to put on a brand new set of garments consistent with our new life in Christ. Paul writes, "Clothe yourselves with the new self, created according to the likeness of God in true righteousness and holiness" (Ephesians 4:24).

Paul changes the images somewhat, but not the intent in Romans 12:2, where he writes, "Do not be conformed to this world, but be *transformed* by the renewing of your minds." "Put off" is parallel to "not be conformed to this world." "Put on" is parallel to "be transformed by the renewing of your minds." There are two words for "form" in Greek. The first one is the root of "*con*form," which is *schēma*, from which we get the word *scheme*. This refers to the external, changeable form. *Schēma* has to do with outwardly blending in, like a chameleon adapting its skin to the flora and fauna. Instead of conforming outwardly we are to be transformed from within. The root of "*trans*form" is *morphē*, from which we get the popular image of *morph*. This has to do with the "inward and real transformation of the essential nature of a person." Ironically, this word has slipped into our popular vocabulary in association with computer-generated images. On the screen we can watch the gradual transformation of a man's face into that of a woman's; one *morphs* into the other.

Literally the term here is *metamorphosis*. This has to do with becoming a new you, not just on the outside but a new, unchangeable inner character. Whereas *schēma* is adapting to the external and fleeting fashion of this world, *metamorphosis* describes the process of a caterpillar becoming a butterfly. The caterpillar spins the cocoon and within it becomes a new creature.

A couple of paragraphs ago I did not tell you the whole story about the transformation of Scholl Canyon from a landfill to a golf course. I only played golf once on that transformed course. For emanating from below the thin layer of topsoil was a nauseating stench. All I could think of when standing on the putting greens was that just below my feet was a bubbling chemical caldron. The landfill had been *schematized*, but it had not *morphed*. A superficial change occurred, but there was no permanent transformation from within. A true transformation would have meant a removal of the rubbish to be replaced by clean soil. This is why Paul constantly connects transformation with the images of "putting off" the old nature and "putting on" the new nature (Ephesians 4:17-32 NIV).

For Paul, the fully devoted, reproducing disciple is one who has grown to reflect the character of Jesus in his or her life. The goal of transformation is to remove all that reflects the old, sinful self, while the scent of Christ permeates the whole being from the inside out. Maturity for Paul is our readiness to have Jesus reflect his nature through every aspect of our being.

If this is the goal, how did Paul help people grow toward maturity or Christlikeness? His parental model can be broken into a series of roles that assist a believer to move from infancy to adulthood. The discipleship process parallels the way parents must adjust how they exercise their role to grow their children into responsible, caring, empowering adults (see table 5.1).

Table 5.1. Paul's parental empowerment model

Life Stage	Life Stage Need	Disciple's Role	Paul's Role
Infancy	Modeling and direction	Imitation	Model
Childhood	Unconditional love and protection	Identification	Hero
Adolescence	Increased freedom and identity formation	Exhortation	Coach
Adulthood	Mutuality and reciprocity	Participation	Peer

Developmental Stage One: Imitation (Infancy)

Paul combines his parental self-understanding with a call to the Corinthians to imitate his life. He views his relationship to them as a father to his "beloved children." He was instrumental in bringing about the spiritual birth of many of the Corinthians: "In Christ Jesus I became your father through the gospel." Then Paul draws out the natural implications: "I appeal to you, then, be imitators of me" (1 Corinthians 4:15-16). In Paul's day fathers were expected to model appropriate behavior and be copied by their children. "Regard your father's conduct as the law and strive to imitate and emulate your father's virtue."[7]

The word *imitate* here is *mimeomai*, from which we get the English word *mimic*. *Mimeomai* is used in a number of places (1 Corinthians 11:1; Philippians 3:17; 1 Thessalonians 1:6-7; 2 Thessalonians 3:7, 9), accompanied often by the word *typos*, which is translated variously as "example," "model" or "pattern." In 1 Corinthians 11:1 Paul qualifies his previously unqualified admonition to imitate himself by adding, "Be imitators of me, *as I am of Christ.*" In other words, his converts were to imitate the evidence of Christ in him. Why doesn't Paul simply say, "Imitate Christ"? Why does he place himself between Christ and the Corinthians? When I first read these exhortations to self-imitation, my thoughts were, *Paul, how can you say such a thing? You arrogant so-and-so, how conceited can you be?* But as my understanding of the ways God developed, I realized Paul was espousing good incarnational theology. God embodies his presence. He came to us fully in Jesus. Then he placed his life in his followers, who become reflections of him. This is the way God has chosen to work—putting up life next to life.

Imitation has the sense of following the lifestyle of another. Paul says to the Philippians, "Brothers and sisters, join in imitating [*mimeomai*] me, and observe those who live according to the example [*typos*] you have in us" (Philippians 3:17). He adds that he, along with his coauthor, Timothy, serve as their models (*typos*). *Typos* is derived from the word meaning "to strike," the mark of a blow or the impression left. A hammer blow on a piece of wood leaves an indentation. A signet ring pressed against wax leaves an impression, a seal. In other words Paul and Timothy's lifestyle provides the mold for the Philippians.

What exactly did Paul expect these churches to become? Was he seeking plastic replicas of himself? Did he expect everyone to have his go-for-broke, single-minded personality? Maybe he expected everyone to get on the road and suffer as an apostle? Was Paul urging that they follow his combative style? This is an important question, since some disciple-making emphases seem to demand superficial replication of the habits and mannerisms of a dominant personality. A generation ago I could easily tell the followers of a particular disciple maker because they kept three-by-five cards in their pockets. They were taught that a disciple was a ready learner and must have the capacity to capture an insight or quotable quote in a moment's notice. This is mild compared to the cultlike characteristics of extreme hierarchical models. Some have promoted a chain-of-command approach that says the one being discipled must have all decisions ratified by the discipler because the discipler is the voice of God to them. Is this what Paul had in mind when he said, "Imitate me"?

We don't need to speculate about what Paul meant when he called people to imitate him as he imitated Christ. When Paul met with the Ephesian elders in Miletus, he gave a clear description of what he thought was worth emulating (Acts 20:17-38). When Paul arrived at the port city of Miletus during his second missionary journey, he sent for the elders of the Ephesian church to offer one last word of encouragement. Prior to their wrenching goodbye, Paul reminded them of his model while he was with them. What did he emphasize? His life was one of humility and tears, enduring the hardship of the plots of Jews that dogged this former Pharisee wherever he went. He remained focused on the core message of the gospel, not compromising its call to repentance, whether that was in public or from house to house. His sole concern was that he might complete the work that Jesus had assigned him. What does Paul want them to imitate? I think Paul might summarize what he would have us imitate like this: "Just as I am willing to die to myself so Christ might fully shine through me, do so yourselves. I am fulfilling the assignment Christ has given me; you do so as well. Be all that you are to be in Christ."

When Paul calls for Christ to be formed in us, he wants us to be the best *us* that God designed us to be. C. S. Lewis has addressed this issue powerfully. We might think that we are to relinquish our lives to Christ and then Jesus blots out our unique personality in order to make us all alike in him. Lewis reminds us that the opposite is true.

> The more we get what we now call "ourselves" out of the way and let Him take us over, the more truly ourselves we become. There is so much of Him that millions and millions of "little Christs," all different, will still be too few to express Him fully. He made them all. He invented—as an author invents characters in a novel—all the different [people] that you and I were intended to be. In that sense our real selves are all waiting for us in Him. It is no good trying to "be myself" without Him. The more I resist Him and try

to live on my own, the more I become dominated by my own heredity and upbringing and surroundings and natural desires. . . . It is when I turn to Christ, when I give myself up to His Personality, that I first begin to have a real personality of my own.[8]

As a discipler, Paul believed that the way he lived his life in Christ was worth being caught and modeled by others. This is a necessary element in our ability to invest in others as well.

Developmental Stage Two: Identification (Childhood)

Loving parents tie their welfare and happiness to the welfare and happiness of their children (see table 5.1). In this regard Paul had the heart of a parent when it came to the welfare of his spiritual children. Paul's ability to enter into the lives of his converts allowed them to turn around and fully identify with him. In chapter three I described the impact that Don had on my life during my impressionable college years. I was soft clay in search of someone to help shape my life purpose. I desired to be like Don because I identified with him. Yet I identified with him because he gave himself to me. When I recall times with Don, I see in my mind's eye engaging conversations seated side by side on a bench next to a tennis court or across from each other at a picnic table in a park. What I remember from those times is being allowed into the heart of this man. He shared not only his love for Jesus but also those tender and tough places where Jesus needed to remove the dross of his life. The passion I observed in Don made me want to be like him.

Imitation becomes motivating through identification. "Identification is the process in which a person believes himself to be like another person in some respects, experiences the successes and defeats as his own, and consciously or unconsciously models his behavior after him. . . . The fact that there is emotional involvement with the other person distinguishes identification from mere imitation."[9]

Emotional identification is engendered in the discipleship relationship by the discipler making a life investment. Paul identified with and entered fully into the lives of those he served. Paul used maternal and paternal images to convey the connection of his life with their welfare.

Paul boldly embraced feminine images to convey his emotional con-nection with those he longed to bring into Christian adulthood. Perhaps the most unusual maternal image is when Paul refers to the Galatians as "my little children, for whom I am again in the pain of childbirth until Christ is formed in you" (Galatians 4:19). I don't know what Paul knew about labor pains. He most likely had heard the wailing of women in labor and thought this agony was analogous to his feelings about the Galatians. On the long night when our daughter was born, my usually immaculately kept wife had no concern about her appearance. Her sweat-soaked brow had straightened out the curls on her forehead. Her body buckled into a V-shape every five minutes. I have long since tried to forget the sounds that ejaculated from deep down. Then came the pronouncement of the early morning, "This is the worst night of my life!" Just so, Paul vicariously endured the pangs of childbirth as he engaged the Galatians in their messy process of growth in Christ.

When we turn to Paul's first letter to the Thessalonians, he continues the maternal image, saying, "We were gentle among you, like a nurse tenderly caring for her own children" (1 Thessalonians 2:7). A good case can be made that *nurse* here is "nursing mother," which makes sense when coupled with "caring for her own children." There is nothing like the understanding of a mother's love. The low point of my adolescent development came in the transition from elementary school to junior high. I lived in a constant state of fear of failure in the classroom, fear of loss of friendships and fear of not performing athletically. My world was not a safe place. Many a night I would sob myself to sleep. Watching a son go through this broke my mother's heart. She could not stand to see her child in pain. I have warm recollections of bedside talks and soothing poems meant to bring comfort to my troubled soul. So Paul was to the Thessalonians. He draws on the image of Moses taking up the people of Israel into his bosom "as a nurse carries a suckling child" (Numbers 11:12). This gentle side of Paul is not our usual image.

Eugene Peterson captures this section well in the *Message*: "We were never patronizing, never condescending, but we cared for you the way a mother cares for her children. We loved you dearly. Not content to just pass on the Message, we wanted to give you our hearts. And we *did*"

(1 Thessalonians 2:8). It was not a matter of dropping gospel bombs and then moving on to the next town. Churches often invite in a guest speaker who comes to give a prepackaged message, but one does not get the sense that such guest speakers have come to give themselves. As a pastor I had a dream of a biannual teacher or prophet-in-residence who would come for a month and live among us. The hope was to not only get their impassioned message but also live with their heart. I wanted more than the in-and-out speaker. The dream died because numerous invitations yielded only one person willing to make such a commitment. Paul went and stayed. He gave himself, not just his message. He could not conceive of the message apart from its being incarnated through his being.

Paul balances his maternal self-description within a few verses by adding, "As you know, we dealt with each one of you *like a father with his children*, urging and encouraging you and pleading that you lead a life worthy of God, who calls you into his own kingdom and glory" (1 Thessalonians 2:11-12). Wise parents know to treat each one of their children as individuals. What motivates one child may be demotivating for another. Whereas an agreeable temperament may be characteristic of one child, another may be constantly pressing the boundaries. One child may have an artistic bent, whereas another has the genetic code of an accountant. Paul says that he dealt with "each one of you like a father." Discipling is about respecting the individuality of a disciple and assisting his or her uniqueness to blossom in accord with God's design. In the developmental process a watchful parent can already see in the childhood years the particular inclination of each child.

Paul selects three verbs to describe the nature of his fatherly discipling relationship with the Thessalonians. Each of these words conveys a different motivational strategy that depends on the individual state of growth and disposition. "We dealt with each one of you like a father with his children, urging . . . encouraging . . . pleading."

The word for "urging," *parakaleō*, is the same descriptor that Jesus uses for the Holy Spirit when he says, "I will send you another counselor, comforter, advocate, helper, or encourager" (see John 14:16; 16:7). We have all these different translations because, no one English word is adequate to capture the various nuances of the term. Literally the word means "to come alongside to help." Paul came alongside, urging them, sometimes bringing comfort, at other times acting as their cheerleader and still other times exhorting them to live up to their calling.

Coupled with urging, "encouraging" (*paramytheomai*) probably means to be encouraged to continue in the course they are on. It carries the sense of "to build up, or to give a reason for hope." The Christian life can be discouraging when we battle our inner demons and the hostile world. We need hope to carry on.

The root of "pleading" (*martyreō*) here is "witness" or "martyr." The word could just as easily have been translated "charging." As a coach might give the impassioned speech to fire up his or her players, so there are appropriate times for disciplers to call the best out of those they are investing in. Paul needed to say on occasion, "Get out of your comfort zone and take some risk in service to Jesus."

Paul did not guard himself against disappointment. He made himself fully vulnerable to the despair that comes when a disciple disappoints. Love requires identification, not self-protection. At the childhood stage of growth, disciples need to know that their welfare is another's deepest concern.

Developmental Stage Three: Exhortation (Adolescence)

The adolescent stage of discipleship is very much like the adolescent stage of a teenager (see table 5.1). During adolescence a critical issue is building confidence so that teens can blossom into their own persons. This occurs by allowing them to learn by trial and error. Parents limit the amount of rescuing, while offering support and consolation as needed. In other words, adolescents grow up by facing the consequences of their actions.

The image of a coach is an appropriate one for this stage. The coach is in the privileged position of helping people to see the potential they didn't know was there. Tom Landry, the legendary coach of the Dallas Cowboys, defined coaching as "making men do what they don't want, so that they can become what they want to be."[10] This is why Elton Trueblood proposed the image of player-coach as the best modern metaphor for the equipping pastor. "The glory of the coach is that of being the discoverer, the developer, and the trainer of the powers of other men. This is exactly what we mean when we use the Biblical terminology about the equipping ministry."[11]

In 2 Timothy, generally considered Paul's last-known correspondence, Paul melds the image of coach and father. Paul conveys in this final letter that the end of his ministry is imminent: "The time of my departure has come" (2 Timothy 4:6). Paul's agenda is to ensure the transmission of the gospel to the next generation. What the Lord has allotted for him to do was complete. So he is thinking about effecting the transition to those that have been in the battle with him. Paul's leg of the race is almost over. But before he receives his reward, he must pass the baton.

One of the persons to carry on in his absence is his beloved son in the faith, Timothy. You get the sense that there were few people in Paul's life who held the place of affection as did Timothy. True, Paul was Timothy's spiritual father, but my guess is if Paul had the choice of a biological son, it would have been Timothy. "To Timothy, my beloved child," he begins 2 Timothy. In his first letter to Timothy he addresses him as "my loyal child." To the Corinthians Paul wrote that he was sending them Timothy, "who is my beloved and faithful child in the Lord" (1 Corinthians 4:17).

The natural order of things is that faith is passed from parent to child. Every son or daughter longs to receive the blessing of his or her father. About a month after my father's death in 1994, I went on a two-day silent retreat, seeking some space to process my emotions in the aftermath of my parents' deaths, which occurred within a month of each other. I found myself drawn to Paul's second letter to Timothy. All of my life I had wanted my father to be in the position to offer his blessing and exhortation to carry on the faith. Now I knew with finality that day would never come. There was a sense that I had missed out on the natural order of things.

Oh, how I envy Timothy. Paul is the coach-father exhorting Timothy to live up to his calling. Paul gets to the core of his intent when he says to his son, "Carry out your ministry fully" (2 Timothy 4:5). Paul follows up that plea immediately with his own example: "I have fought the good fight, I have finished the race, I have kept the faith" (2 Timothy 4:7). Paul's message to Timothy is "You do the same!" As I see it, 2 Timothy is a motivational letter. Read this letter and list all the different ways Paul employs to motivate Timothy, and you would not miss much of the content. All of this variety of motivational means is designed to say one thing to Timothy in the adolescent stage of development: Become the person God has designed you to be.

It is human nature to move toward comfort and avoid pain. We want to live a quiet and peaceable life and to be left alone and insulated from other people's problems. Our sense of urgency dissipates, and we fail to remain on high alert. We lose our focus, and our aims become fuzzy. We need settings where the coach can get in our face. All too often I have watched myself and others slowly turn down the temperature to where we become lukewarm and insipid. We need purifying and refining contexts where the best is continuously called out of us. Humans follow the law of entropy; we wind down, and our energy dissipates unless the poker stokes the coals of our lives to stir them up again.

Developmental Stage Four: Participation (Adulthood)

The goal of the discipling process is to arrive at maturity (see table 5.1). Regarding the goal of parenting, the Balswicks say: "God's ideal is that children mature to the point where they and their parents empower each other."[12] Mutuality marks the stage of maturity. Parents get to the point where they can learn from their children. "Reciprocal giving and receiving is an indication of a mature relationship [between parents and children]."[13] My wife and I are at the enjoyable stage of relating to our married daughter, who has charted her life direction in medicine. She enjoys instructing her aging baby-boom parents in things medical. We consult with her about our aches and pains. We laugh together at our constantly falling for the promises of various anti-aging products that play on our fears of getting older. She has incorporated our values into her life trajectory. We have come to the point of letting go and have become adult partners with our daughter and son-in-law.

Mutuality and partnership marked the adult stage of Paul's ministry. While working with those in the early stages of infancy and childhood in the faith, the discipler is much more directive, and invests and serves as an illustration of the way things are to be. The adolescent stage of growth is marked by exhorting the person to become all that God intended him or her to be. An increasing amount of freedom and experimentation is expected. At the adult stage, learning becomes a mutual process of upbuilding. Paul treats the Romans as adults when he writes, "I am longing to see you so that I may share with you some spiritual gift to strengthen you—or rather so that we may be mutually encouraged by each other's faith, both yours and mine" (Romans 1:11-12). Paul dignified the Romans by saying he was not coming only to give to them but to receive from them as well. Healthy relationships are mutual. This does not imply that maturity levels are equal. But no matter what one's maturity level is in Christ, there is something to offer as well as receive. Paul, no matter his stature in the faith, would never outgrow the need to receive the benefit of some spiritual gift the Romans could offer.

In his ministry Paul viewed himself as a partner and colaborer with others in the gospel. We have a significant list of names of people Paul shared with in mutual labor in the gospel: Timothy, Titus, Epaphroditus, Silvanus, Priscilla, Aquila, Euodia, Syntyche, Onesiphorus (see, for example, Romans 16). Though in terms of authority Paul was an apostle, he restrains himself from a heavy-handed use of that authority. For example, when he writes to Philemon about his runaway slave, Onesimus, Paul addresses Philemon as a "dear friend and co-worker" (Philemon 1). Urging Philemon to receive back Onesimus, Paul says that as an apostle he could exercise that authority in the form of a command, but instead, out of respect for Philemon, he appeals on the basis of love.

Paul avoids hierarchical language in relationship to those who share in the ministry of the gospel. Missional relationships are collegial. In 2 Corinthians 8:23 he refers to Titus as "my partner and co-worker in your service." The term *partner* derives from the familiar *koinōnia*, meaning "that which we share in common," often translated as "fellowship." "We are in this together" is Paul's message. Paul identifies Epaphroditus as "my brother and co-worker and fellow soldier" (Philippians 2:25). Later in this same letter, Paul is concerned about unity between two women, Euodia and Syntyche. He says of them that they "struggled beside me in the work of the gospel, together with Clement and the rest of my co-workers" (Philippians 4:2-3). Though Paul is not shy about calling those stuck in infancy to grow up, he does not stress the hierarchical nature of the dis-cipling process. And though there are differences among us in maturity levels, stressing these differences is not helpful.

Paul's parental discipling model always had the goal of encouraging people to become all they were intended to be in Christ. Paul's desire was for completeness in each believer, meaning fulfilling a person's unique, God-given design. Making people replicas of himself was not on Paul's agenda. He did not see himself as the sage on the stage but the guide by the side. Paul's missional model of discipleship conveyed that we are in partnership to take the gospel to those who desperately need to hear of the love of God. When mission predominates, partnership and mutuality mark the relationship between a leader and God's people.

Paul's parental discipling model was layered. On the foundation of imitation came identification, marking the infancy and childhood stages of faith. As disciples began to develop their identity, Paul exhorted them to grow into their potential. Then, finally, Paul expected people to grow to maturity by entering into full participation with him in the gospel.

Summary of Jesus and Paul's Model

Jesus intentionally called a few to multiply himself in them. He intended his ministry to become the ministry of the Twelve and be the means by which he extended himself to the world. To prepare the Twelve, Jesus followed a *situational leadership* model, adjusting his leadership style to the readiness of his followers. As Jesus adjusted his leadership to match the readiness of the disciples, he also changed styles to provoke them to the next level of growth. Jesus shifted his roles from living example to provocative teacher to supportive coach and finally to ultimate delegator. Though Paul's language and images differed, his goal and process mir-rored the model of his Lord.

We come to the "so what" section of our reflection. How do we take this biblical vision and translate it into a church-based model of disciple making? This is where we have usually failed. Many Christian leaders have a working knowledge of what I have covered in these last three chapters, but we need to take the biblical imperative and make it workable. This is the connection that the next chapters will make.

PART THREE

MULTIPLYING
REPRODUCING
DISCIPLESHIP
GROUPS

Church-Based Strategy for Disciple Making

6

LIFE INVESTMENT

It's All About Relationships

We have come to the critical point in our exploration of how to grow self-initiating, reproducing disciples of Jesus Christ. We need to make a practical connection between the way Jesus and Paul made disciples and how we carry it out in our ministries and churches. And yet I remain mystified. After twenty-five years of holding disciple-making workshops in local churches and teaching pastors at the doctoral level, it still seems we have rarely adopted the relational, developmental model of making disciples right before our eyes in the New Testament. Frankly, like any author I want to sell books, but it is discouraging that this book is still relevant. Why isn't the model of disciple making clearly practiced by Jesus and Paul so commonplace and second nature that a book like this is unnecessary?

What are we missing? We seem to be missing the hinges. Hinges that allow a door to swing freely on the door frame and therefore to function the way it is designed to do. The *frame* in our analogy is the biblical vision just described in chapters three through five. The *door* is our ministry. But without hinges, the door merely leans against the frame and doesn't accomplish its intended purpose. In order for our ministries and churches to grow reproducing disciple makers, three hinges need to be attached.

Before I describe these three hinges, the subject of chapters six through eight, let's briefly remind ourselves what keeps the door (ministry) disconnected from the frame (biblical model). One pastor's journey is representative of the stories I have heard over the years. In his own words,

After thirteen years on the staff of a major campus ministry, you would have thought that I had understood the importance of making reproducing disciples, but I had not. When I became a senior pastor in 1983, because of my many duties I lost the focus on making disciples. Having come out of a highly evangelistic ministry, it was all about more and more decisions for Christ. But if any disciples came from that, it was purely incidental, not intentional. For the first twenty-seven years of this ministry, you would have thought that I had been exposed to the "flashy thing" from the movie *Men in Black*. Then in 2008, at the prompting of Willow Creek's REVEAL Survey, we did our own. After all, we couldn't deny how poorly we were doing at making disciples. We were doing all those things that "good" churches are supposed to do. The professional ministry staff focused on engaging worship, preaching the Word, making sure we had programs in place to nurture and connect people, developing small groups, offering hospitality, raising money to build first-class facilities and the like. But with all that activity, the data was staring us in the face. We were not seeing people on any significant scale being transformed into disciples of Jesus, and could count on one hand motivated lay leaders who were discipling others.[1]

We will hear from this pastor again, but at this stage he is fairly typical of the way a pastor carries out his or her role. On the one hand, we want to grow as big of an audience as possible. Numbers are the game. It tells us whether we are being successful. In addition, the pastoral-care model creates an air of dependency. The pastoral staff does ministry, and the people are the recipients. Even if there is a concerted effort to gather people in educational communities and small groups, or send out occasional mission teams, the idea is still to grow people in Christ internally. People become end users. There is little to no expectation that they will adopt of lifestyle of discipling others. Sure, there is the rare exception we can point to, but it is the exception that proves the rules. People come for what they can get, not for what they can give. After all, the ultimate givers are those we pay to do ministry to or for us.

So how do we turn the corner and create a culture of disciple making so that growing self-initiating, reproducing disciples is normative? We need to put three hinges in place to connect the frame to the door.

In this and the next two chapters we will explore three foundational principles on which to build a process that leads to an intergenerational multiplication of fully devoted followers of Christ.

- The first hinge is *relational life investment*. How do we shift from an emphasis on making disciples through programs to making disciples through relationships (chap. 6)?

- The second hinge is *multiplication* through the generations. How we can disciple people to maturity and *reproduction* (chap. 7)?

- The third hinge is *transformation*. What are the necessary relational conditions to create an accelerated process of growth of reproducible microgroups (chap. 8)?

Disciples Are Made Through Relational Life Investment

Disciple making is not a six-week, ten-week or even a thirty-week program. Adding components that make a program more rigorous or time-consuming does not produce disciples. As we noted in chapter two, programs tend to be (1) information or knowledge based, (2) focus on one preparing for the many, (3) require regimentation or synchronization, and (4) foster an atmosphere of low personal accountability.

How does the need for intentional disciple making usually make it onto our radar screen? Perhaps you can identify with one or more of the following scenarios:

1. *Recycling the saints.* You begin to notice that your leadership pool is too small to fill the established leadership roles. So we use the same people time and again. It is like multiple tours of duty for soldiers. Can we keep wearing out the same folks? But who is in the pipeline? Is there even a pipeline?

2. *Empty ministry slots.* A new ministry year is upon us and the scramble is on to find teachers to tackle the rambunctious sixth-grade class. Or perhaps we have reached the ceiling of ministry development. For

example, all of our small groups are closed to new participants because we are not developing new leaders to form new groups.

3. *Tired of putting on the show.* After ten years of weekend ministry production, you are exhausted. Meeting the ministry needs of consumer Christians is draining. And what do you really have to show for it besides a bigger audience, which only increases the pressure of producing a bigger and better show? And the more we have catered to consumer desires it seems the less transformation into Christlikeness we have seen.

Whatever brings the issue into focus, you recognize that you have a discipleship-making deficit. Typically, the solution is to form a committee to come up with a discipleship program. The committee scours the national landscape for a discipleship program that has had success. This usually means you are looking for a system and a curriculum that can be easily implemented in order to provide an accelerated solution to the ministry-recruitment problem. The program is located. The prepackaged curriculum is accepted as is or adapted to your particular ministry, and then it is implemented. With great fanfare and high expectations the new program is announced as the tool that will lead people into victorious Christian living and a willingness to serve in ministry. The church leaders hope against hope that disciples will be multiplied and the talent pool expanded. Yet what all began with great promise turns to disappointment because the same 20 percent who are already overcommitted sign up for this as well. Thus the saints get recycled one more time. The size of the ministry base is substantially the same as it was prior to the promising program. Figure 6.1 depicts this approach.

Figure 6.1. Program-based discipling

What is the missing ingredient in this program approach? The priority of relationship. Don't get me wrong. Some programmatic elements are necessary. I am not opposed to curricula, complete with sequenced knowledge, skills acquisition, spiritual disciplines and doctrinal content, but for transformation to occur all this must be processed in the context of a relational commitment.[2] Jesus serves as our model. He said to those who would be his disciples, "Follow me and I will make you fish for people" (Mark 1:17). In association with me, Jesus says, I will provide what you will need to fulfill the call I place on your life. This same relational emphasis needs to be at the heart of our disciple-making strategy (see fig. 6.2).

Figure 6.2. Relationship-based discipling

The Power of Personal Invitation

What distinguishes *program* from *relationship*? It starts with the way we issue the invitation. We have failed to appreciate the power of personal invitation to be with others on an intimate basis over time. My challenge to the church and Christian community is to return to the primacy of this invitation as we walk together toward maturity in Christ. When I consider initiating a new discipling relationship, it is preceded by prayer to discern the persons the Lord would place on my heart. Let's follow Jesus' model here. Jesus took the initiative to call his disciples to himself after spending the night in prayer; discipling relationships should be formed on the basis of a prayerful invitation by the one initiating the discipling relationship. In offering the invitation to potential partners, I say something to the effect of "I have been praying about something I would like you to consider. I am putting together a new group whose express purpose it is to help each of us become better followers of Christ. I would like to invite you to meet with me and at least one other person weekly for the purpose of becoming all that the Lord intends us to be. My role is to be on this journey with you. I need a group like this in my life as well. So in a sense I am doing it for me. As I was praying about this relationship, the Lord has put *you* on my heart. Would you be willing to prayerfully consider joining with me and one or two others as we grow together to become better disciples of Jesus?" I want the person to whom I am making this invitation to know that they have not been randomly chosen out of the church directory but someone the Lord has laid on my heart with a settled conviction over time. In chapter nine we will reflect on the qualities we might look for in a discipling partner.

The following is another illustration of an invitation to discipleship. (Though this was a mass invitation to a number of women, it serves as a model of intentional discipleship in a relational, transparent setting.)

Dear Friends,

I am reaching out looking for a group of ladies who would like to be in an accountability group with me. What are we going to be accountable for? For daily spiritual practices and looking to live like Jesus every day.

This isn't a coffee or gossip group or even a Bible study group. I don't have a special book to read, just a strong desire to know and follow Jesus better and to have some ladies I can discuss this journey with. People I can trust the big things with, mostly my dreams and my failures. A place filled with love and trust, not comparison or judgment. I'm stuck right now spiritually, and maybe you are too.

So, if you are looking to go deeper with God and in relationship to others, I hope you will consider joining me. Yes, it is one more thing to do each week, *but oh how it could change the other hundred things you have to do.* Making God a priority, truly, is what I'm looking for. That's what I need. If you need that too, let me know.

Love you all, Cassie

How does this approach differ from the usual church program? Instead of inviting people to a program or class for which they sign up, attend and complete their assignments, they are invited into a relationship of mutual love, transparency and accountability. Can you see how different this kind of invitation is? It is the difference between a pastor, staff member or key lay leader standing in front of the congregation making a general appeal to sign up for a program versus looking an individual in the eye with prayerful conviction, and inviting them into a personal relationship.

Of course, discipling relationships contain programmatic elements, such as a curriculum, but the relational dynamics are primary. How does relationship differ from a program? Let's contrast relationship with the four characteristics of programs as previously identified:

First, discipling relationships are marked by intimacy, whereas programs tend to be focused on information. We can easily fall into thinking that transferring truth leads to transformation. In a church I served, the assumed strategy when I arrived was to hire pastors with the appropriate theological credentials and have them teach correct doctrine to groups of people in a classroom setting. If we could get people to assent to core beliefs, such as justification by faith alone, then the job was complete. Right belief made us right with God. But there seemed to be minimal concern for transformation into the character of Christlikeness.

Alicia Britt Chole captures this difference between information and intimacy:

> Program was safer, more controllable, and reproducible—less risky, less messy, less intrusive. It seemed easier to give someone an outline than an hour, a well-worn book than a window into our humanity. How easy it is to substitute informing people for investing in people, to confuse organizing people with actually discipling people. Life is not the offspring of program or paper. Life is the offspring of life. Jesus prioritized shoulder-to-shoulder mentoring because His prize was much larger than information; it was integration.[3]

Second, discipling relationships involve full, mutual responsibility of the participants, whereas programs have one or a few who do on behalf of the many. One of the main limitations of a program setting is the lack of responsibility of the participants. If the presenters have done all the preparation, what is required of those receiving the teaching? As a worshiper sitting in a pew, there is no accountability for the truth you are hearing. Yet in a discipling relationship the partners share equal responsibility for preparation, self-disclosure and an agenda of change. This is not about one person being the insightful teacher and the others passively receiving the insights of the teacher, whose wisdom far exceeds their own. Maturity levels in Christ will vary, but the basic assumption is that in the give and take of relationships, the teacher and the recipients can vary from moment to moment.

Third, discipling relationships are customized to the unique growth challenges of the individuals, whereas programs emphasize synchronization and regimentation. A program usually has a defined length. A person commits to ten weeks, and then is done. Churches often follow the academic calendar, beginning a program in September, when school starts, and completing it in June in time for summer vacation. But program assumes that everyone who proceeds through it must do so in lockstep fashion. A discipling relationship cannot be confined by such artificial constraints. Discipling relationships necessarily vary in length of time, because no two people grow at the same speed. It is not a matter of a regimented march through the curriculum but an individualized approach that takes into account the unique growth issues of those involved.

For example, in one of my recent microgroups, the four of us by age occupied successive decades. A month after our group's inception Billy got married. Nine months later their first child arrived. At the inception of this group Billy was questioning the wisdom of being in a group with men who spanned thirty years his senior. He quickly discovered why the group was good for him. Billy needed a place to process his rantings regarding adapting to married life, and then how he could survive as a father of a newborn. Seasoned veterans created a calming influence. Ron occupied the next older decade. Ron's discipleship issue was an inability to trust God. He was the eldest of six children with a father who was a raging alcoholic. Ron dealt with unresolved hatred of his father. Our challenge with Ron was to help him grasp that he was an adopted child of the Father through Christ, and he could finally have the parent his father would never be. Climbing up the ladder of the decades we come to Dave. Dave, a seasoned believer, was rightly respected for his deep and gracious faith. Yet after thirty-two years in the insurance business, he sensed that God had something else for him. It was a privilege to pray and process with him as he went through a major life transition—out of a predictable life into a risky ministry adventure. I was on the decades' top rung. In the midst of our time I was diagnosed with virulent prostate cancer. I needed to lean on these men, with whom I could share both my fears and my hope. Though we followed the structure of a discipleship curriculum, our relationships remained paramount. Programs have a prescribed length; discipling relationships don't. Relationships adjust to the needs and dynamics of what is happening in the lives of the people at the moment.

Fourth, discipling relationships focus accountability on life change, whereas programs focus accountability on content. Growth into Christlikeness is the ultimate goal. The measure of accountability in programs tends to be observable behaviors such as memorizing Scripture, completing the required weekly reading and practicing spiritual disciplines. Though all of these are vital, in a discipling relationship the accountability focuses on learning to "obey everything that [Jesus has] commanded" (Matthew 28:20). For example, there is a huge difference between knowing Jesus taught that we are to love our enemies and actually loving our enemies. Discipling relationships are centered on incorporating the life of Jesus in all we are in the context of all that we do. (See chapter eight for a fuller discussion on life-change accountability.)

The Attractiveness of Relationships

Invitations to programs seem impersonal. A program is something the church tries to get people to come to "for their own good." An invitation to relationship, by contrast, is experienced differently. In an impersonal world, people hunger for intimacy, personal care, deep friendship and spiritual bonding. This is particularly true for men. Studies have shown that men generally have acquaintances but few if any intimate friends. Two out of ten males seem to have meaningful, open and safe relationships in which both parties trust and are committed to each other. In contrast, six out of ten women enjoy this type of relationship.[4] When men are invited to join others to explore what it means to follow Jesus, I find a motivating hunger.

One of the men in a church I served spoke for many when he wrote,

For many years I had been searching for a safe place in which I could explore, with a group of other guys, the questions and issues that were coming up in my walk with the Lord. On earlier occasions, I had enjoyed Bible studies that were aimed at either couples or larger groups of guys. Neither one of these settings had really stretched me to examine my faith in a personal way and find out who I was in Christ. As a result of this spiritual hunger, I began looking for a small group of fellow believers who wanted to develop a deeper relationship with our Lord through a regular study of His word. In short, I was looking for some men with whom I could be honest, accountable, and vulnerable.[5]

Build Slowly, Build Solidly

If we make relationship the priority, we will need to change from our shortcut approaches to making disciples. Underlying the programmatic mindset is a view that disciples can be made quickly. We are always looking for an instantaneous solution to our recruiting problems or growing people in Christ. In short, we would love to be able to microwave disciples. Robert Coleman puts the key issue in stark focus: "One must decide where he wants his ministry to count—in the momentary applause of popular recognition [program splash] or in the reproduction of his life in a few chosen ones who will carry on his work after he has gone? Really, it is a question of which generation we are living for."[6]

We have succumbed to the temptation to seek "the momentary applause of popular recognition." We judge our success by the number of people in the worship center. We hold a pastor's Bible study as the means to getting God's Word into people. Or we adopt the latest program that seems to produce results somewhere else. Behind these efforts is the mentality of the instantaneous.

Coleman, following Jesus' model, points us toward *building slowly and building solidly*. A significant portion of a leader's time should be given to a "few chosen ones who will carry on their work after they are gone."[7] This means having enough vision to think small. An effective builder of people looks ahead five to seven years for the discipleship results. Yet our inability to delay gratification is a major contributing factor to our discipleship deficit. At a seminary in Manila I taught Filipino pastors about the need to have a long-term vision of disciple making. As I was speaking, I became aware of a murmur spreading through the class. I stopped my lecture and said, "What did I say? What's going on?" They explained to me that in the uncertainty of their political climate, when a regime change can occur at any moment, thinking long term seemed laughable. I pushed back. I said, "You will, most likely, be pastors in the same locations as you are seven years from now, so you might as well invest for the long haul." It appears that thinking long term is not any more common in the Philippines than it is in the West.

This change to a longer-term developmental mindset is a critical turning point if we are to develop a disciple-making culture. Waylon Moore in his classic book *New Testament Follow-Up* captures this mindshift, "A decision that our ministry will be intensive, rather than extensive, will change our whole life. Quality begets quantity. It takes vision to train one person to reach the mass."[8] He goes on to say that it takes three to five years of sustained effort for the multiplication impact of a growing network of reproducing disciples to have an obvious influence on the climate of a congregation. It takes that long for the awareness of this kind of growth to emerge in the consciousness of the broader community. So our challenge is, Are we willing to invest for the long haul? Or will we fall into the short-term quick fixes that have produced the discipleship deficits to date?

In the model I will propose, three or four people journey together for twelve to eighteen months while they grow toward maturity and are equipped to disciple others. As this relationship comes to a close, each person is challenged to invite two or three others into the same walk of faith and then reproduce, and so on. Over the five-to-seven-year period of multiplying discipleship triads or quads, eighty to a hundred or more people will have been carefully groomed in the context of an intimate relationship. This number of self-initiating, reproducing disciples has a tremendous impact on the climate of a ministry. It takes only 10 to 20 percent of a congregation to set the tone for the whole. Invest in those who will set the pace for the rest. At the same time, one's leadership base is greatly expanded. Key leaders who are willing to assume responsibility for ministry or initiate new ministries come from this discipleship harvest. Most of us never see that kind of fruit because we do not have that kind of vision. We are too oriented to short-term results, and therefore we try to create shortcuts that don't produce the growth we want. Because we have not focused on the principle of *building slowly, building solidly*, we consistently serve churches of overgrown spiritual children.

Discipling Defined

What is included in a discipling relationship? At the heart of a discipling relationship is one or more believers who invest in each other in order to grow to maturity in Christ. Bill Hull defines discipling as "the intentional training of disciples, with accountability, on the basis of loving relationship."[9] The International Consultation on Discipleship established the following definition of discipleship: "We define Christian discipleship as a process *that takes place within accountable relationships over a period of time* for the purpose of bringing believers to spiritual maturity in Christ."[10] The distinctive nature of discipling is that it involves a relational investment intended to create an atmosphere of growth to maturity in Christ.

Here is my working definition of discipling: "Discipling is an intentional relationship in which we walk alongside other disciples in order to encourage, equip and challenge one another in love to grow toward maturity in Christ. This includes equipping the disciple to teach others as well."[11]

Let's break this definition down a phrase at a time:

Intentional relationship. At a most basic level, *intentional* means that the discipling partners will meet on a regular time schedule, preferably weekly. The opposite of intentional is sporadic or haphazard. "Let's get together when we can" is at the other end of the spectrum. *Intentional* also implies "purposeful." A relationship is established for the purpose of "growing together toward maturity in Christ." This relationship has a covenantal character. The parties commit themselves to mutually agreed standards that give shape to the relationship. Being with one another in intimate relationship is the primary means through which Christlikeness will be produced.

Walk alongside other disciples. "Walk alongside" is carefully chosen to convey that this approach to disciple making is *non-hierarchical*. The intent is to create a mutual, egalitarian interchange, where life rubs up against life. For reasons I will explain in chapter seven, this definition proposes a peer-mentoring approach to discipling rather than "a more experienced follower of Christ shares with a newer believer"[12] or a "teacher-student relationship."[13]

Three qualities characterize this reciprocal discipling relationship.

First, in discipling relationships we *encourage* one another. We need safe places to freely explore who we are in Christ in a positive, grace-filled environment. The word *encourage* is the same one Jesus uses for the Holy Spirit, the *paraklētos* (often translated "encourager") who comes alongside to help. Discipling partners are the Holy Spirit's instruments used to affirm all that is special in one another as God releases us to be his unique creations.

Second, growing into Christlikeness involves *equipping* our daily lives with spiritual disciplines that place us in the presence of Christ's shaping influence. The word *equip* implies that part of the process will include practicing skills, disciplines, behaviors and patterns that give structure to being a follower of Jesus. Included in transformation is the reordering of habits.

Finally, in the context of a covenantal relationship, there will come times when our partners *challenge* us to follow through on commitments we have made, or strongly urge us to take risks. Just as I challenged Eric to pursue a mission opportunity in the midst of his intended world tour (see the introduction), so there will be times when others need to challenge us. *Challenge* implies that there is accountability rooted in a mutual covenant. Giving others permission to speak into our lives is a frightening step for most of us.

In love. It is important to wrap all of what is done in love for those with whom we are on the journey. Love and trust are inseparable. As soon as we suspect that someone is attempting to control us or who speaks to us in anger in order to punish or harm us, we will become guarded and withdraw. Love is the womb in which Christ can be formed in us. Chicks best emerge from the egg to new life when they have received the warmth of a nesting hen.

To grow toward maturity in Christ. The goal of a discipling relationship is to become whole, complete or mature in Christ. This means that no one partner has arrived, but all are on a common journey toward being fully grown in Christ. I stress peer accountability because no one person can serve as a complete model for another. In fact, a sign of maturity is the ability to learn from the least likely source.

Equipping the disciple to teach others. The ultimate goal is reproduction. Included within our understanding of maturity is that the disciple has internalized the value of multiplication and gained the confidence and capacity to lead someone to Christ and walk alongside that person toward Christlikeness. The expectation of reproduction needs to be implanted from the inception of the covenantal relationship. It then needs to be reinforced through extended time together. The biggest hurdle is moving people from receivers to givers. This turn of the heart to an outward reproduction focus is critical. This involves hand-to-hand combat with our enemy, who does not want a lifestyle of reproducing disciple makers to take hold!

Discipling Incarnated

A number of years ago I received one of those letters that redeems all (or, at least, most of) the disappointments in ministry. I share a portion of this letter because the author illustrates so powerfully the importance of long-term discipling relationships. To understand the letter, let me recreate the context. My first ministry position out of seminary was with college students at the University of Pittsburgh. The church I served was located across the street from the student dorms. We had developed a fairly extensive outreach to about three hundred students who attended our midweek service. At the center of the ministry was a leadership team of about forty students who led outreach Bible studies, which we called "action groups," on the college campus and were being discipled by our five full-time staff. The letter I received was from a former student who was a freshman at the time I was called from Pittsburgh to serve a church in California. I barely knew this student, yet she wrote to commend the ministry model she had experienced while at the University of Pittsburgh. What makes this letter all the more compelling is the time lag between when I left this ministry and when she wrote. My departure from Pittsburgh to California occurred in March 1977; her letter is dated April 1985.

Dear Greg,

My name is Jane Smith [not her real name]. I was just starting to get involved in the church fellowship when you were called to California. I was so impressed with the few times I heard you teach, but more than anything else I was drawn into the love that the fellowship had for you and each other. To an outsider at the time, like myself, one saw such a deep love that I know was prayerfully developed. The term discipleship was living.

Long after you left, your leadership materials were being used—I was trained by [she mentions three student leaders] who were a part of the inner circle that I admired and the Lord used in my life.

After graduating from the University of Pittsburgh with degrees in child development/child care, my husband and I were led to start a Christian center [in Pennsylvania]. The Lord has done miracles step after step in this ministry, and we're so excited about it! We started with a preschool program and now have started a Christian school, adding a grade each year.

We feel that by applying biblical principles and models, we can minister to families in the area. In any case, because of the model I experienced at Pitt, the center is focusing on small, quality, long-term relationships with families.

Now, the reason I'm writing—I realize now the commitment you had at Pitt and how much time and effort you so selflessly poured into those guys. I appreciate you and your gifts because I feel like I am the fruit of your fruit! And praise the Lord more fruit is being produced! I appreciate your model because of our ministry, and how easy it is to give yourself out and spread too thin and not accomplish much. If you ever question the Lord about your work at Pitt— please think of me and know how much the Lord used you there. So . . . I just wanted to say thanks!

P.S. I guess you will understand this letter—I just pray that someday someone will write to me expressing their faith in our Lord, and that perhaps my obedience was somehow related to their growth.

Jane underscores all the points I have been trying to stress in this chapter. Let's highlight her insights.

The term **discipleship** *was living.* In the community of believers Jane saw the embodiment of discipleship through the love of the community for its leaders and for each other. Love was the magnet that drew her to this body. Jesus had something to say about this: "By this everyone will know that you are my disciples, if you have love for one another" (John 13:35). Jane observed this truth in Christian community probably long before she read it in her Bible.

Trained by members of the inner circle. The leadership team was the inner circle. The leaders met every Wednesday evening for training and support in their ministry. Each member of the student team was being discipled and encouraged by staff as they led outreach Bible studies on campus, and each also invested in a few others. In this setting these were the junior and senior college students Jane admired and who gave themselves to her. Often an inner circle is experienced as a clique that keeps people out, yet this inner circle drew her in.

Long after you left. A discipling or training model has a much greater chance of outliving a primary leader than does one built around a leader's personality. The test of leadership is what happens after the leader moves on to his or her next ministry. The ministry was infused with a philosophy of discipleship reproduction, which was not dependent on me. Jane was a freshman at the time of my departure. I had a minimal relationship with her, yet the relational and developmental structure was in place to carry her through four years of college.

Because of the model I learned. In establishing a ministry to families, Jane and her husband had decided to focus on "small, quality and long-term relationships." I could not have picked three better adjectives to describe the discipling process. She and her husband had chosen depth over breadth.

The fruit of your fruit. I have publicly and privately read this letter innumerable times in the last thirty years, and I never come to that line without a catch in my throat and moisture in my eyes. Even though I had no personal relationship with this young woman, she recognized that the discipling chain had passed through the generations and that she was in a sense my spiritual granddaughter. What a joy it is to know that the reproduction takes place when those you have discipled have caught the vision and have the skill and heart to disciple others.

Jane captures what has been the fatal flaw in ministry and a major cause for undiscipled believers: "how easy it is to give yourself out and spread too thin and not accomplish much." This is the epitaph that could be written over the life of many a pastor or Christian leader. In our attempt to be equally available to all and avoid being accused of having favorites, "small, quality, long-term relationships" for most pastors do not seem to be a priority.

We need to have enough vision to think small. This requires that we shift our way of thinking and acting to produce lasting fruit in key individuals who will in turn teach others. We must exorcise the instantaneous from our thinking. Put off the old ways of being all things to all people. One of the key leadership roles is to have at all times a few we are investing in, preferably weekly, who are being brought to maturity in Christ in a relational context. The results of this longer-term strategy will be a broadening leadership base of self-initiating disciples, multiplication of fruit beyond our initial efforts and a ministry that will long outlive us.

> Essentially, the pastor's first priority is to so invest himself or herself in a few other persons that they also become disciplers and ministers of Jesus Christ. It is to so give oneself to others and to the work of discipling that the New Testament norm of plural leadership or eldership becomes a reality in the local congregation. In other words, it is to bring the ministry of all of God's people to functioning practical reality.[14]

When it comes to assessing the value of real estate, the mantra is "Location. Location. Location." A mansion in a poor rural area can be purchased for a fraction of the same home with an ocean view. When it comes to making disciples, the mantra should be "Relationship. Relationship. Relationship." Programs give the illusion of productivity. We can count the number of graduates who have gone through our systems. But are they able to invest their lives meaningfully in others so that these can "teach others as well" (2 Timothy 2:2)?

David Platt states the relational challenge:

Making disciples is not an easy process. It is trying. It is messy. It is slow, tedious, even painful at times. It is all these things because it is relational. Jesus has not given us an effortless step-by-step formula for impacting nations for his glory. He has given us people, and he has said, "Live for them. Love them, serve them, and lead them. Lead them to follow me, and lead them to lead others to follow me. In the process you will multiply the gospel to the ends of the earth."[15]

In chapter seven we will explore how microgroups are the ideal environment to create a multiplication movement, and in chapter eight we look at four key ingredients in the discipling relationship that create an atmosphere of accelerated transformation.

7

MULTIPLICATION

Through the Generations

The paradigm shift question that has served as the driving force behind this book is, How can we grow self-initiating, reproducing, fully devoted followers of Jesus Christ? The most befuddling challenge contained in this question, and the conundrum few have solved, centers on *reproducing*. Perhaps an even greater challenge than growing fully devoted followers of Christ is growing fully devoted followers who reproduce. Multiplication is the key to fulfilling the Great Commission, "Go therefore and make disciples of all nations" (Matthew 28:19).

Any credible definition of discipling should contain within it the concept of reproduction. Gary Kuhne writes, "Discipleship training is the spiritual work of developing spiritual maturity and spiritual *reproductiveness* in the life of a Christian."[1] Kuhne says this same thing from the angle of one who is setting the disciple-making pace: "A multiplier is a disciple who is training his spiritual children to *reproduce* themselves."[2] We must raise the bar so there is a new normative expectation. To train a disciple is to train a reproducer.

I confess: figuring out how to grow reproducers was one of the great frustrations of my ministry.

For a couple of decades I lived with deep frustration: those I invested in were not discipling others. My usual approach was to meet with someone one-on-one on a weekly basis. My hope was to encourage a deepening faithfulness to Christ and to empower the individual to reproduce in another, and so on, thus multiplying effectiveness. Our agenda would include mutual sharing about the growing edges of our faith; learning and practicing the basic spiritual disciplines, such as the devotional elements of prayer, Bible study and Scripture memory; exploring the implications of obedience to Christ in the spheres of family, work, church or inner struggles; studying a foundational book such as John Stott's *Basic Christianity*; and coaching the person in a church-related ministry. But . . . no multiplication.

I was stymied. For fifteen to twenty years I labored with a discipleship model that amply demonstrated the popular definition of insanity: Doing the same thing over and over again and expecting different results. I thought what I needed to do was refine or improve the same thing I was doing. If I tried harder, prayed more regularly and streamlined my approach, the results would be different. Multiplication charts (like fig. 7.1) acted as law, condemning me in my failure where others must be succeeding. After all these years I have concluded that the model I was pursuing was faulty. To paraphrase Dallas Willard, perhaps the reason I was getting these results was not in spite of my approach to discipling but because of it.

YEAR DISCIPLER	EVANGELIST	DISCIPLER
1	365	2
2	730	4
3	1,095	8
4	1,460	16
5	1,825	32
6	2,190	64
7	2,555	128
8	2,920	256
9	3,285	512
10	3,650	1,024
11	4,015	2,048
12	4,380	4,096
13	4,745	8,192
14	5,110	16,384
15	5,475	32,768
16	5,840	65,536

Figure 7.1. Evangelistic addition vs. discipleship multiplication

I was forced to ask some probing questions, which you too might be asking. Why don't we see more reproduction? What obstacles get in the way? Is it a matter of a low commitment? Is it the fault of leaders who are afraid to ask for more? Have we succumbed to the comfort of Western consumerism, and therefore our Christianity is only about what God can do for us? These are contributing factors. In chapter two we looked at a number of causes for the low estate of discipleship. But here my question is more focused: What are the barriers to reproduction? Why don't our intentional discipleship models seem to produce multiplication?

Some thirty years ago I stumbled on an approach that has led to a significant reproduction rate in an ever-growing network of church-based disciple-making strategy. My problem, in my estimation, was that I had become transfixed by a biblical icon, which fueled a nonreproducible model.

The Usual Biblical Model (Paul and Timothy)

The biblical paradigm that usually serves as the basis for our understanding of discipling is Paul and Timothy's relationship. These two are linked together as the prototypical unit. Preachers regularly urge every Paul to have a Timothy or even more commonly for every Timothy to seek out a Paul to be a mentor. Our definitions of discipling are generally influenced by the unspoken assumption that the Paul–Timothy model is the universal paradigm. Paul Stanley and J. Robert Clinton support this one-on-one model of the more mature believer discipling the less mature: "Discipling is a process in which a more experienced follower of Christ shares with a newer believer the commitment, understanding and basic skills necessary to know and obey Jesus Christ as Lord."[3] Lurking in the background of Keith Phillips's definition is the Paul–Timothy model: "Christian discipleship is a teacher-student relationship . . . in which the teacher reproduces the fullness of life he has in Christ in the student so well, so that the student is able to train others to teach others."[4]

In linking Paul and Timothy as *the* biblical model, assumptions are made about what this kind of relationship should entail:

- older person with a younger person (like a parent-child relationship)
- more spiritually mature with less spiritually mature (usually associated with an age difference)
- teacher-student relationship (learned with the unlearned)
- more experienced with the less experienced (passing on distilled wisdom)
- one in authority over one under authority (hierarchical)

The Usual Model of Disciple Making

Because of the imprint of the Paul–Timothy model, we unquestioningly assume the one-on-one relationship as our reference point in discipling relationships. But with the hindsight of thirty years of discipling in microgroups, the following are my reflections on some of the limitations of the one-to-one discipling dynamics.

1. In the one-on-one relationship, the discipler carries the responsibility for the spiritual welfare of another. The discipler is like the mother bird who scavenges for worms to feed to her babies. With their mouths wide open, the babes wait in their nest for the mother bird to drop in the morsels. The discipler is cast in the role of passing on his or her vast knowledge to the less knowledgeable. This puts pressure on the discipler to perform and be the focal point in the relationship. In this model, in order to disciple another, one must have arrived at some undefined state of spiritual maturity. Unwittingly we have created a role few will feel qualified to apply for. Instead of the discipler enjoying a freedom or ability to be his or her self, an imposed perfectionism fosters self-consciousness.

2. The one-on-one relationship sets up a hierarchy that tends to result in dependency. As the line of authority is emphasized, an unspoken reliance is built that is difficult to overcome. Though the Timothies (people in the receiving position) might be appreciative, they will have difficulty seeing themselves in the giving position. After all, the dynamic created is that they are the young, immature ones. They are to receive from the fount of wisdom of the one who has walked longer in the faith. The gulf between the Paul and the Timothy is exacerbated when the relationship is between pastor and parishioner. Pastors are perceived as qualified to disciple others because they have years of biblical and theological training and the vocation to go with it. How could the disciple possibly make up for his or her lack of formal education!

3. One-on-one relationships limit the interchange or dialogue. I liken the one-on-one discourse to a Ping-Pong match. It is back and forth, with the discipler under pressure to keep the ball in play. The conversation must progress to some higher plane. As a discipler I found that I did not listen as carefully as I should have, because I was thinking about some wise counsel or insight I might provide, given my role. In other words, the dialogue is often not a dynamic interchange because it is limited by the number of participants.

4. One-on-one relationships create a one-model approach. The primary influence on a new disciple becomes a single person. This in itself can be limiting and tends to skew the development of the disciple. The parameters of the discipling experience are defined by the strengths and weaknesses of one individual. Do we really want our life to be the sole model of Christian discipleship? I don't think so. Each of us is just one expression of Christ working in us.

5. The one-on-one model typically does not reproduce. If the one-on-one model does reproduce, it is rare. Only self-confident, inwardly motivated persons can break the dependency and become self-initiating and reproducing. This was the crux of my frustration. Over considerable time, I was investing in one person, but if multiplication was a major goal, I wasn't seeing a return on the investment.

I concluded that we have inadvertently held up a hierarchical model of discipling that is nontransferable. As long as there is the sense that one person is over another by virtue of superior spiritual authority, few people will see themselves as qualified to disciple others. We may tout this as a multiplication method, but it contains the seeds of its own destruction.

As a result of my experience I propose a nonhierarchical model that views discipling as a mutual process of peer mentoring. In order to avoid the dependency trap, the relationship needs to be seen as side by side rather than one person having authority over another.

The Alternative Biblical Model

A biblical alternative to the Paul–Timothy model will serve as the basis for a side-by-side relational approach to disciple making. Though the relationship between Barnabas and Paul didn't end on the best of terms (see Acts 15:39), it still serves as "iron sharpens iron" peer discipling, which I find healthy and consistent with Paul's view of his relational partnership in mission (see chap. 5). As we track Barnabas and Paul's connection through the book of Acts, we will observe that the lead position constantly changes. The shifts depend on their gifts and the ministry circumstance.

Barnabas makes his first appearance at the end of Acts 4. Barnabas, meaning "son of encouragement," is a nickname given to him by the apostles (Acts 4:36). He was born Joseph and was a Levite from Cyprus. Barnabas had sold a piece of property and entrusted the proceeds to the apostles so they might use the money for the needy in the church community. The next mention of Barnabas occurs in Acts 9, when he becomes linked with the firebrand Saul—turned apostle Paul. The disciples in Jerusalem were rightly skeptical of Paul's conversion. They feared it was a ruse or masquerade feigned to infiltrate the ranks of the apostles. But Barnabas vouched for the genuineness of Paul's life change and witnessed how he had put his life on the line in Damascus, speaking boldly about Jesus (Acts 9:27).

Barnabas and Paul parted company for a considerable time until they were reunited in Antioch (Acts 11:19-30). Barnabas had been sent from headquarters in Jerusalem to investigate the strange rumors that not only Jews but even Gentiles had received the grace of God in Antioch. Having gained a reputation for being able to spot the genuine article, Barnabas was their man. Barnabas affirmed that the same manifestations of grace rested on these Gentile believers as was evidenced in the chosen people. After sizing up the situation Barnabas recognized that the teaching task was greater than he could handle by himself. Though years had passed by now, he remembered God's call on Paul, who was commissioned by the Lord to be an apostle to the Gentiles. Barnabas tracked Paul down in his hometown of Tarsus; Paul had exorcised his legalistic Pharisaism and replaced it with freedom-in-grace theology. Barnabas was the tool that the Lord used to get Paul into the game.

Barnabas and Paul labored side by side in Antioch until the Holy Spirit spoke to the worshiping leaders, confirming that Barnabas and Paul were to be sent on what we now call Paul's first missionary journey (Acts 13:1-3). It is interesting to observe how the order of the names—Paul and Barnabas, Barnabas and Paul—change in the varying circumstances of their work. While Paul emerges as the primary spokesperson, it is evident that he does not eclipse Barnabas. Sometimes the order is Barnabas and Paul (Acts 13:2, 7; 14:12, 14; 15:12, 25) and sometimes it is Paul and Barnabas (Acts 13:42, 46, 50; 14:1; 15:2, 22, 35).

The point of the shift from Paul–Timothy to Barnabas–Paul as the biblical model for disciple making is the need to change from a hierarchical approach, which creates dependency, to a peer mentoring model, which has much more promise of empowering multiplication. At this point you may rightly object, *But what about modeling? Isn't it important for someone who has walked longer in the faith to be an example and teacher for those who are beginning? Haven't you spent an entire section of this book helping us see that Jesus invested in a few and that his life was the primary means of influence used to shape the Twelve? You have told us that Paul even had the audacity to say, "Imitate me as I imitate Christ." Now you seem to be backing away from modeling as the foundation of disciple making.*

I am saying that placing the discipler in positional authority over the disciple is not necessary for modeling to occur. Let's return to the examples of Jesus and Paul. What was Jesus' authority based on? Certainly not any recognized manmade position he held. The Greek word for authority is *exousia*, which means "out of being." Jesus spoke as one having authority, not as the scribes and Pharisees. Jesus' authority was recognized by the ring of truth of his words, backed by the consistent quality of his life and underscored with a demonstration of power. The only human title Jesus acknowledged was rabbi. Jesus did not have authority because of his association with a recognized rabbinical school or the imprimatur of a highly regarded rabbi. And Paul's authority was not so much in his position as apostle but in his passionate desire to die to himself so that Christ would come alive in him. The qualities in his life, not the credentials he held, made his life worth imitating.

The person leading a discipling microgroup need not hold a position of authority, except as the convener and keeper of the covenant the group members have mutually agreed on. Authority is more a matter of quality of life than of position. In other words, in a relational context influence will naturally occur within the relationship. The depth of one's spiritual life and insight, the evident passion to serve Christ and the application of Scripture to life will naturally flow out in the dynamic interchange. Authority is placed in the mutual covenant the participants agree to. If the qualifying mark of those in the microgroup is the desire to be all that Christ wants them to be, whatever their starting point—pre-Christian to veteran—then there is an environment for transformation.

The Alternative Model of Disciple Making

As the alternative to the one-on-one model, I propose triads (3) or quads (4), which I have been calling microgroups, as the ideal size for a disciple-making group. We will explore in chapter eight why this size maximizes the conditions that accelerate growth

It was not my great foresight that led me to change from the one-to-one to a microgroup. As I mentioned in the introduction, it came as a result of a ministry experiment in an academic program. I had written an earlier version of the curriculum now titled *Discipleship Essentials* and wanted to test its usefulness. Since this experiment became the basis for a final project for a doctor of ministry degree, my project adviser suggested that I try it out in different contexts in order to examine the variable dynamics. We agreed that I would use the material in the traditional one-on-one mode, in a small group of ten and also in a group of three. I was caught off-guard with the life-giving dynamics I experienced in my first triad. How could adding one person change the entire feel of what happened in that relationship? The goal had not changed. It remained seeing the Lord grow self-initiating, reproducing, fully devoted followers of Jesus. The only difference was the direction and structure provided by a curriculum and the addition of one individual, yet it all seemed so much more alive!

Here is my best take on why microgroups are energizing, joy-filled and reproductive.

1. There is a shift from unnatural pressure to natural participation of the discipler. When a third person is added to a discipling relationship, there is a change from the discipler as focal point to a group process. The discipler in this setting is a fellow participant. Though the discipler is the convener of the microgroup, he or she quickly joins the journey together toward maturity in Christ. The responsibility that comes from being the focal point is lessened, since the emphasis is on mutuality. The discipler prepares and interacts with the content as a peer rather than as an authority whose insight is to be weighted more heavily because of the leadership position.

2. There is a shift from hierarchical to relational. The microgroup naturally creates a come-alongside mutual journey. The focus is not so much on the discipler as it is on Christ as the one all are directing their lives toward. Even as a pastor I found that though the relationship may have started with a consciousness that I was the Bible answer man, within the first few weeks the others allowed me to be another disciple who, like them, was attempting to follow Jesus. A significant part of the discipling relationship is to share our personal challenges of faithfulness. When my partners saw that I too was having to deal with the real stuff of life, the polished halo faded and I was allowed to be a real person.

3. There is a shift from dialogue to dynamic interchange. In my initial experiment with triads, I often came away from those times saying to myself, *What made that interchange so alive and dynamic?* The presence of the Holy Spirit seemed palpable. Life and energy marked the exchange. As I have come to understand group dynamics, one-on-one is not a group. Only as we add a third or fourth do we have the first makings of a group.

In a one-on-one relationship, there are only four possible combinations of communication. Each individual has a unique perspective and an opinion about the other person's perspective. When we add a third party, the number of possible interplays of communication increases to ten. Each of the three persons has two relationships (2 x 3 = 6); then each person has a relationship with the other two as a pair (1 x 3 = 3), thus making nine possible configurations. But there is a group personality, which is the tenth and most dynamic aspect of the threesome. The addition of a third person multiplies the possible configurations of communication and creates a corporate personality. (I will let you do the math if it is a quad.)

4. There is a shift from limited input to wisdom in numbers. The book of Proverbs speaks of the wisdom that comes from many counselors (Proverbs 15:22). To this end I have often found it life-giving to have people at varied maturity levels. Often those who may be perceived as younger or less mature in the faith provide great wisdom or a fresh spark of life. In one of my triads Ken was perhaps the least likely source of spiritual inspiration. His partners were me (a pastor) and Glen (a former Baptist pastor), whose knowledge of Scripture exceeded mine. Ken, a retired dentist, had come to a warm relationship with Christ well into his sixties, but he lacked confidence, especially in his knowledge of Scripture. In the first weeks of our sessions Ken slumped in his chair with his head bowed. The bottom edge of a discipleship workbook was propped on his lap and hugged to his chest as if he were afraid for anyone to see what he had written. He reminded me of a third grader who did not want to make eye contact with the teacher in order to avoid getting called on.

Only a few weeks into our relationship Ken was diagnosed with cancer and had to begin weeklong in-hospital regimens of chemotherapy every third week. So every third week our discipleship sessions shifted from my office to the chapel on the hospital floor where Ken was receiving his treatments. Even though this adversity was a setback for Ken, it seemed to open up a surge of God's grace flowing into his life. The once insecure neophyte was now eagerly teaching us about how God's presence was available in times of testing. The hospital staff informed me that Ken had made quite an impression during his weeks during his treatment. They told Glen and me that Ken had become the unofficial chaplain. Instead of remaining in his room attached to his drip bag he roamed, pulling his rolling pole behind him, from room to room bringing joy and encouragement. His demeanor radiated the warmth of Christ's love. The teachers (Glen and I) were now being taught. We were sitting at Ken's feet, hearing a man speak wisdom beyond his Christian years.

5. There is a shift from addition to multiplication. For the better part of three decades, I have observed a significant reproduction rate (approximately two-thirds) through the triad model of disciple making. One of the joyful memories seared into my brain was my last Sunday as associate pastor at the church where I first developed a network of triad relationships. As I was leaving the church property that Sunday, I ran into Kathy on the patio under our sprawling Morton Bay fig. She cradled in her arms the spiral-bound notebook I had titled *A Disciple's Guide for Today* (the precursor to *Discipleship Essentials*). She giddily told me that Kay had invited her into a discipleship triad, which was going to begin that next week. My first thought was, *What a joy it is to know that a ministry of discipling and reproduction now has a life of its own and is going to continue to multiply long after old "what's-his-name" is forgotten.* That joy was further enhanced since I had nothing to do with discipling Kay, who had invited Kathy into her next triad. Since these initial efforts I have seen the same reproduction occur in two subsequent churches where I was senior pastor and executive pastor of discipleship respectively. When I was senior pastor in the Silicon Valley, we titled our newsletter *Discipleship Bytes*. This quarterly publication printed the names of those participating in the multiplying microgroups. My heart was warmed when I saw on the list spiritual grandchildren and great-grandchildren who were far removed from the original microgroups that got the whole process going.

In summary, a microgroup encourages multiplication because it minimizes the hierarchical dimensions and maximizes a peer-mentoring model. By providing a discipleship curriculum specifically designed for this intimate relationship, it creates a simple, reproducible structure that almost any growing believer can lead. Leadership in these groups can be rotated early on, since the size allows informal interchanges and the curriculum provides a guide to follow.

One-to-One Mentoring Relationships

In my discipling workshops participants often object to my perceived attack on the one-on-one model. They tell stories of how their lives have been influenced by an individual who invested in them. So let me take a moment to both affirm the value of these one-on-one relationships and contrast them with an intentional disciple-making relationship.

What people are usually alluding to is some form of mentoring. Three types of mentoring relationships are quite common and work best in the one-on-one setting:

- *Spiritual guide or director.* "Spiritual director" has become associated with a trained individual who has the skills and spiritual sensitivity to assist a directee to discern what and how the Holy Spirit is working in a person's life.

- *Coach.* The role of the coach is to ask powerful, clarifying questions that force the one being coached to reach deep inside to find empowering answers.

- *Sponsor.* A sponsor generally has positional or spiritual authority within an organization who can provide the resources to develop a mentee's rising influence.

Though a discipling relationship is a type of mentoring, it is distinct from one-on-one mentoring roles. First, in most mentoring relationships the mentee seeks out or initiates the request for a mentor. As one who currently has a few mentees, the mentees always have requested that I be their mentor. The agenda is set by the needs and desires of the one being mentored. In a discipling relationship, the discipler, following Jesus' model, initiates the relationship and defines the agenda. The expressed purpose of discipling relationships is to lay the foundation of spiritual practices, core doctrinal teaching, transformative character qualities and outward ministry focus, so a person has the tools necessary to disciple others. In others words, discipling comes with defined content to be mastered, internalized and then passed on.

One of the goals of a discipling ministry is to grow an expanding network of people who have adopted a lifelong lifestyle of discipling others. The last of five elements in the *Discipleship Essentials* covenant, which the participants commits to, is "to continue the discipling chain by committing myself to invest in at least two other people for the year following the completion of *Discipleship Essentials.*" This is not a program element but a way of life. A person with a *program* mentality completes the program and then asks, "What's next?" What's next for multipliers is to look for others they can walk alongside in order to assist them in becoming links to the next generation. Randy Pope, pastor of Perimeter Church, says he is in his forty-eighth consecutive year of having a men's discipleship group.

In 2000 the movie *Pay It Forward* started a pay-it-forward movement. The movie's story line is that a seventh grade teacher, Mr. Simonet, challenges his class each year "to do something to change the world." Starry-eyed dreamer Trevor McKinney takes the assignment seriously. He comes up with the scheme that challenges each person to do something significant for three others who couldn't do it themselves. In turn, each of the three recipients, instead of trying to *pay back* the favor, would turn around and find three others and *pay it forward* instead. A key moment occurs when Trevor stands at the classroom chalkboard explaining his vision to his classmates while sketching out the multigenerational transmission of these acts of grace. The motive behind discipling others is most certainly unwarranted grace. Freely receive; freely give. We each become conduits for grace received. We demonstrate that we have truly received grace by passing it on. Discipling is *paying it forward*.

Imagine how your church or ministry would be transformed if a culture of paying it forward were normative. What would be the kingdom impact when every believer had the opportunity to be involved in an intensive, year-long relationship with two or three others for the expressed purpose of becoming reproducing disciples of Jesus? Imagine pastors who can relax because they see self-initiating, reproducing disciples searching out those they can invest their life in. Church life would shift from the ministry of professionals to a mobilized body of multipliers.

This more intimate, intentional microgroup environment contains within it the elements for transformation to take place. If the goal is to grow self-initiating, reproducing, fully devoted followers of Christ, we need contexts in which metamorphosis into Christlikeness is a lifelong quest. How do microgroup create transformative contexts? We turn our attention to this subject in chapter eight.

8

TRANSFORMATION

The Four Necessary Ingredients

Without question, the setting where I have experienced the most accelerated transformation in the lives of believers has been in small, reproducible discipleship groups I have labeled *microgroups*. I call them "hothouses of Holy Spirit." Hothouses are heated enclosures that create the right environmental conditions for living things to grow at a rate greater than under natural circumstances. Each summer Alaska becomes its own version of a hothouse. On a trip to Alaska my wife and I gaped at daffodils the size of dinner plates, heard stories about five-hundred-pound pumpkins and witnessed zucchini squash the length of baseball bats. During the summer months in Alaska the sun almost never ceases to shine. Though the growing season is quite short (May through August), the conditions are optimum for accelerated development. I came to see this as a helpful analogy for what happens in a microgroup. Progress in Christian living may have been steady and incremental up to this point, but in a microgroup there is a noticeably quickened pace.

A microgroup is the optimum setting for the convergence of four environmental conditions that create the hothouse effect:

1. transparent trust

2. the truth of God's Word in community

3. life-change accountability

4. engaged in our God-given mission

In a narrative form, this reads: When we (1) open our hearts in *transparent trust* to each other (2) around *the truth of God's Word* (3) in the spirit of *life-change accountability* (4) while engaged in our *God-given mission*, we are in the Holy Spirit's hothouse of transformation.

Let's examine each of these four environmental elements.

Climatic Condition 1: Transparent Trust

We return to the fundamental truth that has been the subtheme in this book: Intimate, accountable relationships with other believers is the foundation for growing in discipleship. What kind of relationship is this? The atmosphere to be fostered in a microgroup is an ever-increasing openness and transparency. In chapter six I quoted a woman who expressed this well, saying she was looking for "people I can trust the big things with, mostly my dreams and my failures. A place filled with love and trust, not comparison or judgment."

Why is transparent trust a key ingredient for continual transformation? Here is the guiding principle: *The extent we are willing to reveal to others those areas of our life that need God's transforming touch is the extent to which we are inviting the Holy Spirit to make us new.* Our willingness to be real with each other is a sign to God that we are truly serious about becoming all he intends us to be.

I can hear the objections. Why is it necessary to reveal ourselves to others? After all, God knows all that there is to know about the state of our heart. We can have a transparent relationship with God. The Lord alone is the one we need to be accountable to. It is nobody else's business what our struggles are as long as we are not trying to deceive God.

Therein lies the problem: deception. Human beings have an almost infinite capacity for self-deception and self-justification. The prophet Jeremiah captured the mystery of the human heart:

The heart is devious above all else;
   it is perverse—
who can understand it? (Jeremiah 17:9)

The IRS received the following note: "Gentlemen: Enclosed you will find a check for $150. I cheated on my income tax return last year and have not been able to sleep ever since. If I still have trouble sleeping I will send you the rest."[1] This man was willing to be honest up to a point—just enough to help him sleep. We need all the tools at our disposal to live in truth about ourselves before God. The apostle John connects our ability to remain in truth and light to our relationships with each other. "If we claim we have fellowship with him and yet walk in darkness, we lie and do not live out the truth. But if we walk in the light, as he is in the light, we have fellowship with one another, and the blood of Jesus, his Son, purifies us from all sin" (1 John 1:6-7 NIV).

Trustworthy. Transparency in our relationships grows in a trust-worthy environment. *Trustworthy!* What an interesting word! Worthy of trust. Trust is not a given but must be earned. Teenagers often say to their parents, "You don't trust me!" If parents were honest, their reply might be something like, "You are darn right. I will trust you as soon as you demonstrate that I can trust you!"

What builds trustworthiness? (1) Trust keeps confidences. Partners do not have to fear that their shared secret or even personal shame will come back to them through some other source. The rule of thumb is what is shared in the group stays in the group. (2) Trust is full of grace. The woman quoted earlier said she does not want "comparison or judgment." When we know we will receive understanding and the accepting heart of God, there will be freedom to be ourselves, warts and all. (3) Trust listens. We will share with each other to the extent that we feel we are heard. Will our partners seek to know more? Will they stay with us, or will they veer off to their own story and stifle self-revelation? (4) Trust is rooted in humility. The humble have no pretense about their own capacity for sin. We come together as broken people. Trust is unshockable. There is nothing that surprises God about us, nor should there be about each other.

Levels of communication. Another way to picture the self-disclosure we are seeking is through the levels of communication.

1. *Cliché conversation.* This is superficial chitchat that focuses on safe topics like the weather, sporting events, local happenings, etc.

2. *Sharing of information and facts.* Talk consists of events, ideas and data, but not really anything personal.

3. *Sharing ideas and opinions.* We are finally entering risky territory because our ideas and opinions can be countered.

4. *Sharing of feelings.* When we share joy and sorrow, gratitude and anger, hope or depression, we are making ourselves vulnerable.

5. *Peak communication.* Openness, transparency, self-disclosure. We are known for who we truly are rather than an image we would like to project.[2]

Our goal is to get to the level of peak communication, which can occur as we proceed through the following stages of trust development.

Stages of trust development. What are some stages or layers of trust development that we must go through to get us to relational transparency? We can compare growing a trustworthy environment to wading into deeper waters. Each successive stage signifies deeper water.

What are the elements that grow transparent trust that will allow us to move gradually into the deep waters of transformation?

- affirmation through encouragement
- walking with one another through difficult times
- being reflective listeners
- confessing our sins to one another

Affirmation through encouragement (sticking our toe in the water). When a microgroup first convenes, we experience anxiety. We are asking ourselves questions: *Will I like these people? Will they be safe to be around? Will they take an interest in my life?* So we begin by sticking our toe in the water to take its temperature.

Anticipating this anxiety, I like to begin my groups with some fun, guided storytelling that will engender laughter. Laughter is the ultimate icebreaker. I often start our first session or two asking each person, depending on their marital status, to tell the story of their courtship (how they met, proposed, etc.), including a humorous incident. If single, I ask them to share about a deep friendship and what makes it special. In addition, I like to have each person share the story of their spiritual journey. We take our time carving out fifteen to thirty minutes for each person to tell about their family of origin, times when they were closest to and further from God, turning points, significant influencers in their relationship with Christ and so on. Our stories foster a much richer understanding of each person.

Trust grows when we experience those in the group as our cheerleaders. In *Restoring Your Spiritual Passion* Gordon McDonald comments on the cleansing and purifying power of a rebuke, saying, "One solid and loving rebuke is worth a hundred affirmations."[3] I like to turn that around and say that we need a hundred affirmations for every loving rebuke. This truth came home to me one Sunday just prior to worship. As I was leaving the restroom I found myself standing next to one of our worship leaders. I thought to myself, *I rarely have the opportunity to express my appreciation to Chris for what he means to the quality of our worship life.* So I said, "Chris, I just want to take this moment to thank you for the way you bring us into the presence of Christ. You truly are a gift to me and to so many others." What caught me off-guard was the intensity of his response. You would have thought that I had told him he had won a million dollars in the lottery. He exclaimed, "Thank you *so* much! I hardly ever hear that!"

As Chris evidenced, in a world that does a much better job of beating us up than building us up, we are starved for honest and meaningful affirmation. Trust is built on the foundation of mutual encouragement. If encouragement is our experience, we are prepared to wade more deeply into the water.

Walking with one another in difficult times (water up to our waist). When we enter a covenantal relationship where we will stay together for a year or longer, we will have the opportunity to address life's highs and lows. Paul captures the rhythm of relationships in the body: "If one member suffers, all suffer together with it; if one member is honored, all rejoice together with it" (1 Corinthians 12:26). This is especially true in a microgroup. There are life circumstances we have no control over, and these circumstances can be devastating. One of the privileges of this intimate relationship is to be able walk with one another during these times. Paul encourages the Thessalonians with these words: "Night and day we pray most earnestly that we may see you face to face and restore whatever is lacking in your faith" (1 Thessalonians 3:10). We gain trust through the faithfulness of partners who sustain us when the bottom has fallen out.

George (not his real name) was the host for our quad since we met around his conference room table in his small law firm. This was the appropriate setting because throughout the entirety of our twenty months together, George lived on the precipice of the demise of his law practice. He brought us into his fear, which he called his "old friend." When he told us his "old friend" was back, we knew exactly what he meant. After a particularly devastating loss in a legal case the end was in sight, and George wrote,

> We have endured great hardship, hoping for a better future. Now it seems that future will not come to pass. I must face the reality that the career I have worked for 18 years is not working. I am 45 years old and must rely on my mom for handouts. I have bills to pay, a car that hardly runs and a crushed spirit. If dreams sustain a man I am in real trouble.

One Thursday morning, our usual meeting time, George shared his concern that he would not be able to fund his employees' paychecks the next day. We of course listened empathetically to his fear, but also like the bed carriers taking the paralytic to Jesus, we lifted George to the Lord's presence. Friday came with no prospects of escaping this disaster. Would he have to finally close his business and declare bankruptcy? The mail arrived around noon. In it was a settlement check from a client that George had long since written off as a delinquent payment he would never see. It was just enough to cover their immediate needs. I know it was a lifeline for George to have these brothers who walked alongside him every step of the way through the tunnel of fear. Now a half a dozen years later, I am happy to report that George's law practice not only survived but now thrives. Welcome to life in a microgroup.

I have been in the trenches with men struggling through long-term unemployment, shaky marriages, runaway children, immanent home foreclosures, various kinds of addictions or life-threatening illnesses, major changes in vocations and the like. Paul instructs us, "Bear one another's burdens, and in this way you will fulfill the law of Christ" (Galatians 6:2). When we have developed a bond with others to the extent that another's concerns have become our own, we are in the deep waters together. It is a rare week that I don't leave my microgroup with the sentiment, *What a privilege it was to be with these men today, for where else would we be able to unload our burdens?*

Being carried by the faith of others is often the way to learn to trust God. I have regularly said to people whose lives have come crashing down, "Let my faith carry you for a while. Some day you will be in a position to return the favor." This is exactly what a discipleship group can do as it builds toward transparent trust.

Being reflective listeners (water up to our shoulders). Nothing builds trust like deep listening. Think of those who have a reputation in your life of being good listeners. When you are with them, they seem to be riveted to your story. They don't just ask the perfunctory questions to make it seem like they are interested in you and then turn the attention to themselves. No, they eagerly pursue you with one insightful inquiry after another. They really want to know what is happening in your life. They have the uncanny ability to make you feel like you are the only person on the planet in that moment.

What if we paid attention to each other like that in our groups? In particular, we want to listen for the way God is moving in our partners' lives. Listening is a particular gift we give when someone is attempting to discern God's direction in their life. In chapter six I briefly mentioned Dave, who had spent thirty-two years in the insurance business. In fact, our microgroup met around the conference-room table in his insurance office. During our time together, Dave began to sense that the Lord was leading him in a radically new direction. He had built up a solid portfolio and was highly regarded in the insurance world. Life was comfortable, but something was stirring. We regularly set aside time to listen to Dave in an attempt to help him get in touch with what was being birthed in him. He was at the stage Bob Buford calls "halftime," when there is the internal shift "from success to significance."[4] In a sense we became spiritual midwives, watching the baby mature to the place where he gave up his safe career and joined an organization that coaches Christian CEOs to live out their discipleship in the business world. Dave was leaping without a safety net. He would be starting over, leaving the predictable and setting off into unchartered territory creating an entirely new means of support from nothing. Dave would credit the microgroup as his listening post where he could test and discern God's voice in his life.

A myriad of choices in our lives need to be sorted through to hear God's voice. God's voice can be drowned out by the din of the world or the confusion that comes from a multitude of options. There is no end to issues where there is need for guidance from the Lord: direction in employment, ethical dilemmas in the workplace, bumps in marital relationships, an errant teen, unsaved family members or neighbors, discernment of God's call or passions of the heart. We need places to sort out these conundrums with people who will stay with us and care long enough to follow through!

When we get this involved in the depths of each other's lives, we might as well get in over our heads.

Confessing our sins to one another (water over our heads). The deep end of the pool of transparent trust is the water of mutual confession of sin and addiction. To get to the deep end we must go through the shallower waters of encouragement, support through life's difficulties and prayerful listening. Only then are we likely to confess our besetting sins to one another.

Few believers have the regular habit or the safe context in which to reveal to another human being what lurks in the recesses of our hearts. Until we get to the point where we can articulate to another those things that have a hold on us, we will live under the tyranny of our suppressed darkness. James admonished his readers, "Confess your sins to one another, and pray for one another, so that you may be healed" (James 5:16). James makes a direct connection between confession and healing. In this context healing appears to be of a physical nature. Yet James believed that the health of our spirit directly affects the health of our body. Much bodily affliction is the result of spiritual or emotional sickness. Transformation into Christlikeness is related to being free from the darkness that can drag us down, and confession is a necessary means to free us from the bondage to sin and addiction.

What is the connection between confession and freedom? Bringing the shame of our guilt into the light before trusted members of the body of Christ can have a liberating effect. Once something is admitted before others, it begins to lose its power to control. Sin flourishes in the darkness, but its power dissipates in the light. In one of my triads, Sam (not his real name) signaled that he had something he needed to entrust to the two of us. His halting voice and avoidance of eye contact, coupled with his nervous and self-conscious demeanor, said that a confession was coming. Sam told us that he had a longstanding obsession with pornography, which was governing his life and affecting his marriage. As his partners on this journey toward wholeness, we assured him of our support and affirmed his courage as he tackled this problem. He stated his intent to join a twelve-step group of others struggling with sexual addiction and his desire to reveal this pattern to his wife. The relief in Sam was palpable. To be known and yet still loved was liberating.

Admission of powerlessness in a strange way begins to reduce the power of darkness. In subsequent weeks we received reports of his commitment to a twelve-step program and the encouraging response of his wife to this struggle. Sam's boldness became an invitation to us to go deeper and to withhold nothing that would get in the way of our obedience to Christ.

Dietrich Bonhoeffer captures the power of confession in his classic *Life Together.*

> In confession the break-through to community takes place. Sin demands to have a man by himself. It withdraws him from the community. The more isolated a person is, the more destructive will be the power of sin over him, and the more deeply he becomes involved in it, the more disastrous is his isolation. . . . In confession the light of the Gospel breaks into the darkness and seclusion of the heart. . . . Since the confession of sin is made in the presence of a Christian brother, the last stronghold of self-justification is abandoned.[5]

We are called to be priests to one another. This means we can speak to another on behalf of God. Some of the most powerful moments I have shared in a microgroup occurred when I could look a brother in the eye after a moment of confession and say, "I want you to know in the name of Jesus Christ you are forgiven!" We get to be the voice of Jesus to one in need of liberation. I have been both on the giving and receiving end of the message of absolution.

Learning to swim in the deep waters of transparent trust is a necessary element for accelerated growth in the Christian life. Learning to swim can be a scary experience. But once we trust the water to hold us up, we can relax and experience its refreshment. Relational transparency is the first necessary condition for transformation.

Climatic Condition 2: The Truth of God's Word in Community

The second climatic condition necessary to produce the "hothouse of the Holy Spirit" is the application of the truth of God's Word in a relational environment. You might be wondering why the truth of God's Word is the second condition? Isn't the Scripture primary? It is, but it needs a context in which to be processed. Bible studies are a staple in most churches. Yet with all the Bible studies there appears to be limited life transformation. So many Bible studies seem to focus on increased information without life application. This is why the atmosphere of transparent trust is so vital if we want God's Word to take root deeply in the soil of our lives.

This application of the Word to life is what I call *truth in community*. We bring our open lives to the Word of God and allow it to do its work in us as we share our stories and journey together. The apostle Paul details the purpose of God's Word, "All Scripture is God-breathed and is useful for teaching, rebuking, correcting and training in righteousness" (2 Timothy 3:16 NIV). Two of the qualities Paul highlights are *rebuking and correcting*. *Rebuking* means to be called up short. It is the Holy Spirit's dagger to the heart. For example, Paul writes, "Do not let any unwholesome talk come out of your mouths" (Ephesians 4:29 NIV). As you read this word perhaps the Holy Spirit brings to mind how you have used sarcasm to cut another down while drawing attention to yourself. The Word exposes. You share this with your partners in confession. Then they help you back onto right path through *correction*. This may entail going to the person you harmed and asking for forgiveness. As it says in Hebrews, "The word of God is living and active, sharper than any two-edged sword" (Hebrews 4:12).

The first characteristic Paul mentions is that Scripture is useful for "teaching." Some would translate *teaching* as "doctrine." I would call it simply reality from God's perspective. A generation ago two Christian prophets, Elton Trueblood and Francis Schaeffer, predicted that we were one generation away from losing the memory of the Christian faith in our culture. They said that we were a "cut flower" society, meaning that the Judeo-Christian foundation had been severed from its root. It would only take time for the flower to droop. We are that generation. On the *Tonight Show*, when Jay Leno was the host, he provided evidence for this loss of memory. One night biblical knowledge was the subject of Leno's "Jay Walking" routine. With microphone in hand, he approached two college-age women with the question "Can you name one of the Ten Commandments?" Quizzical and blank looks led to this reply: "Freedom of speech?" Then Leno turned to a young man: "Who, according to the Bible, was eaten by a whale?" After some contemplation, he blurted, "I know, I know, Pinocchio!" Yes, we have lost much of the memory of the Christian faith in our land.

In our day, we need to teach truth in a systematic way to capture in a holistic fashion the big picture of the Christian life. Following the completion of one of my microgroups, one partner in the group approached me and said,

> I have a confession to make. When you asked me to be in the group, I didn't think I had that much to learn. After all I had been studying Scripture my whole life, having been raised in the home of a pastor where the Bible was central. But I discovered that as I explored the faith in a systematic and sequential fashion, my understanding was much like a *mosaic*. There were entire sections of missing tiles. I now have a much more comprehensive picture how the Christian faith makes sense of it all.

Even this woman, who others would have considered a mature and respected follower of Christ, realized that she had major gaps in her holistic picture of the Christian worldview.[6]

This woman's lack of faith integration seems to be the norm, not the exception. Throughout our Christian journey it is as if we have accumulated puzzle pieces that we have thrown into a box. We accrue tidbits of truth through sermons, reading, devotional resources, wisdom from fellow believers and Bible studies. These puzzle pieces are jumbled together, but not assembled into a comprehensive whole. This is why a good discipleship curriculum is vital; it systematically creates an interpretive picture of God's view of reality (see appendix 3, "The Importance of Curriculum").[7]

Let me encourage you with Mick's story. This is the story of a man who began our discipleship quad with a minimal knowledge of Scripture and confused about the nature of a relationship with Christ. Yet in approximately eighteen months he became a reproducer. I first met Mick when he entered our new members class. He handed me a notebook, which contained ninety-seven single-spaced pages of his comparative study of Roman Catholic doctrine to this new Protestant world he was entering. Seeing Mick's seriousness and integrity, I thought he would be a good candidate for a new quad I was getting ready to launch. Mick, along with Chuck, showed up at 6:30 a.m. for our first meeting in George's law office. At our first session I recall Mick bringing his NIV Study Bible, complete with all the book tabs. As we began to discuss the covenant we were committing ourselves to, Mick interrupted us with an announcement. He placed his hand on the Bible as if he were pledging to tell the truth in court. He said, "You know, I have never opened a Bible." I remember word for word what transpired next. "You mean you have never read it seriously?" I queried. Mick reiterated, "No, I have never opened a Bible." In all the doctrinal study that Mick had done, he had read other people's theology, but never did his own research in the primary source. I thought, *Well, this is going to be a long and interesting journey*. But Mick, jumped in, studied, completed our lessons and memorized Scripture. He had a myriad of questions; we ran down numerous rabbit trails. Getting the concept and reality of being justified by grace in Christ alone through faith was something we had to return to regularly because salvation by works was deeply embedded in him. I tell this story because eighteen months later he was leading his own discipleship group. When we start with very little but have the desire and provide a transferable discipleship tool, a novice can quickly become a reproducer.

The truth of God's Word absorbed in the context of transparent community is the second necessary condition to create the hothouse effect of accelerated transformation.

Climatic Condition 3: Life-Change Accountability

The third environmental element that contributes to creating the right climatic conditions for accelerated growth is *life-change accountability*. In other words, the relationship between those on the discipleship journey is covenantal. A covenant is a written, mutual agreement between two or more parties that clearly states the expectations and commitments in the relationship. Implied in this definition is that the covenantal partners are giving each other authority to hold them to the covenant they have mutually agreed to.

But here is the rub. Willingly giving others authority to hold us accountable is for most Americans a violation of what we hold most dear—our freedom. This may be the most countercultural commitment people make to be a part of a microgroup. In the studies that have been done on the uniqueness of the American character, it has been shown that we value freedom or independence above all else. Freedom is certainly an ideal we have proudly exported to the world, and rightfully so. But there is also a dark side to freedom. Our version of freedom stresses *freedom from obligation*. It was summed up by Robert Bellah in his book *Habits of the Heart* with this sentence: "I want to do, what I want to do, when I want to do it and nobody better tell me otherwise." This can lead us to keep our own counsel and not allow others to speak into our life. Yet to gain self-awareness, which is foundational for growth in Christ, we must allow others to hold up a mirror so we can see ourselves clearly.

Accountability brings us back to the core of what it means to be a disciple of Jesus. A disciple is one under authority. A disciple of Jesus is one who does not leave any doubt that Jesus is the formative influence over our lives. Jesus said, "If any want to become my followers, let them deny themselves and take up their cross daily and follow me" (Luke 9:23). Serious disciples practice being under authority in their covenantal relationships in Christ.

Why a covenant? First, a covenant, complete with clear standards of mutual submission, empowers the leader of the triad to carry out his or her primary role: to be the keeper of the covenant. If there are no explicit, mutually agreed upon commitments, then the group leader is left without any basis to hold people accountable. Without a covenant, all leaders possess is their subjective understanding of what is entailed in the relationship.

Second, covenantal standards raise the level of intensity by setting high the bar of discipleship. One of the failings in the church is that we do not ask people to step up to what Jesus asked. Covenantal discipleship relationships can help us get serious about following Jesus on his terms.

Third, with a covenantal arrangement we invite our partners to hold us accountable. Positive peer pressure leads us to follow through. If we are serious about memorizing Scripture, or if we have committed to practice a scriptural command, the chances of following through are greatly enhanced when we have to give account to our partners.

Fourth, a clear covenant at the outset forces a prospective member of a microgroup to assess whether he or she has what it takes to be in a discipling relationship. Reviewing the covenant is part of the initial invitation to journey together. It is sobering to examine whether one has the time, the energy and the commitment to do what is necessary to engage in a discipleship relationship.

The following illustration of a covenant of mutual accountability is taken from *Discipleship Essentials*. As I am inviting someone into a discipleship triad I talk through this covenant with him or her. My commentary is in brackets.

A Disciple's Covenant

In order to grow toward maturity in Christ and complete *Discipleship Essentials*, I commit myself to the following standards:

1. Complete all assignments on a weekly basis prior to my discipleship appointment in order to contribute fully. [I generally say that it will take approximately two hours per week to complete all four parts of the assignment, plus a variable amount of time to memorize the Scripture.]

2. Meet weekly with my discipleship partners for approximately one and one-half hours to dialogue over the content of the assignments. [To this point, the minimum time commitment is three and a half hours per week, plus travel time to the location where the triad meets.]

3. Offer myself fully to the Lord with the anticipation that I am entering a time of accelerated transformation during this discipleship period. [I want people to expect that the process of growth will have a hothouse effect.]

4. Contribute to a climate of honesty, trust and personal vulnerability in a spirit of mutual upbuilding. [I state that this will be perhaps the most honest and self-revealing Christian relationship they have experienced, and that it will lead to mutual confession. I often ask, "How do you feel about that?" The conflicting feelings of fear and attraction are common.]

5. Give serious consideration to continuing the discipling chain by committing myself to invest in at least two other people for the year following the initial completion of *Discipleship Essentials*. [A part of the upfront agenda is that the disciple is not only growing to maturity in Christ but also being equipped to disciple others. Yet the phrase "give serious consideration to" is used in deference to "I will continue the discipling chain," because the person entering the relationship has, as yet, not experienced a discipling relationship. It's difficult to commit to something not yet experienced, but you can plant the expectation from the outset.]

Climatic Condition 4: Engaged in Our God-Designed Mission

The final condition for transformation is to be engaged in our *God-given mission*. In other words, microgroups are not holy huddles. Though these groups are designed to be safe environments internally so we can "let it all hang out," they are meant to be springboards from which we are sent to serve Christ in all dimensions of our lives. To use another image, microgroups should be *way stations* for renewal and refreshment so we can be sent back into the world to have a kingdom impact.

Though this environment is fourth on the list, it is in many ways the most critical condition. Without a mission, we will not have transformation. I had assumed that if we focus on the first three conditions, then mission or service will be the natural outgrowth. But this would be like eating a sumptuous meal and then being asked to exercise. Resistance is the natural response. But if we reverse this pattern and exercise first, there is increased appetite and hunger. The same is true when it comes to spiritual growth. As we engage in the mission of Jesus, our desire for the Word and accountability is heightened. So the healthy regimen for growth is this: exercise is mission, healthy diet is the Word and accountability to obey it, and rest is the trust of relational transparency.

Being a disciple of Jesus defines our identity. It is who we are. We are always representing Jesus in our lives. To reiterate, as a Christ-follower a friend says of his work, "I am a disciple of Jesus masquerading as a furniture salesman." The classic cult movie *The Blues Brothers* is the story of a couple of ex-convicts and wanna-be-musicians who were trying to raise money for an orphanage. Whenever they were asked about their work, they had a standard response: "We're on a mission from God." The idea of two inept, unworthy human beings on a mission from God was the central joke of the story. But isn't that the point: God has to be joking! Yes, the Lord has condescended to accomplish his mission through us. He says to us, "I have a job for you to do, and you are the one to do it."

The crucible of our transformation is our attempts to be reflections of Jesus in a world that has a mixed response to his life and message. What are some of the ways we express this mission?

- We are called together to share the good news of Jesus through our relational network: work associates, family, neighbors, social associations and so on. In a world where relativism reigns, meaning no truth is absolute, we will encounter pushback when we speak of Jesus as the truth for all. Learning to navigate a world that rejects truth will be a shared discipleship challenge. To make this a regular agenda item for your microgroup, keep a prayer list of all the people God places on your heart so that you can be a link to the good news.

- We are called together to "go make disciples *of all nations.*" Jesus' disciples are "world Christians." This means your group will be in touch with Christ's mission to a culture foreign to yourself. One way to do this is to adopt a "unreached people group" who does not have a church or the Scriptures in their language.[8] Get a copy of *Operation World* or *Pray for the World* and choose a people group to get to know and intercede for. Ask that the Lord's grace would find its way into their hearts and that he would raise up workers for the harvest.

- We are called to assist each other in finding the particular God-designed mission each of us is uniquely fitted for. We were all made for a particular purpose. You can assist each other by asking God to show you the need in the church or the world that God has gifted you to address. To discern the need in the church where you might be called to serve, share with each other how you would complete the following: My greatest concern for this church is _____. To discern the need in the world where God might be calling you, answer the following question: Where does the compassion of Christ in you intersect the brokenness in the world?

As we are engaged in mission we are stretched beyond our own limited resources. When we are thrown back in reliance on Jesus, waiting for him to show up because we are outside of our comfort zone, we are just where we need to be. Then we sense even more the importance of our microgroup. In this group we are refreshed, patched up, encouraged and sent out again to be ambassadors of Jesus.

The Discipleship Difference

What sets the microgroup apart from other relationships that contribute to maturity? Why does this context more than others create an accelerated environment for growth?

Table 8.1 shows it best.

Table 8.1. Power of the discipling model

	Intimacy	Truth	Accountability	Mission
Small Groups	✓			
Preaching		✓		
Teaching		✓		
Discipleship Groups	✓	✓	✓	✓

I have a clear recollection of when the insights contained in this chart were revealed to me. One of the necessary steps to complete the requirements for my doctor of ministry degree was to invite my faculty supervisor,

Roberta Hestenes, to come to the church campus to meet with those who walked with me in this discipleship experiment.[9] As you may recall, the focus of my project was to implement in three contexts a discipleship curriculum I had written: one on one, a small group of ten and a triad. The role of the faculty supervisor was to debrief those who had helped me shape the project and to tease out the discoveries from the different contexts. About ten of us gathered around the conference-room table with a white board behind Dr. Hestenes. Being more than a bit nervous with how the discussion would go, I was delighted with the feedback and the reported impact on lives, especially of those in the smaller discipleship units. As Dr. Hestenes listened and delighted in their report, she saw the power of these discipling units. With excitement she sprang to her feet and drew figure 8.1 on the white board.

She said a small group of six to ten people tends to emphasize fellowship or intimacy, while truth, accountability and mission are secondary. In classroom teaching or preaching, truth content is primary, with intimacy, accountability and mission taking a back seat. The discipling context is transformative, she said, because it brings all four of these elements together in a balanced way.

Every believer or inquirer must be invited into a relationship of intimate trust that provides the opportunity to explore and apply God's Word within a setting of relational motivation, and to make a sober commitment to a covenant of accountability.

What would happen to the health of your ministry five to seven years from now if multiplying discipleship groups proliferated in the church community? I introduced chapter six with Pastor Ralph Rittenhouse's story of how for twenty-eight years he had amnesia regarding intentional disciple making. By his own admission he had lost his way. Intentional disciple making had slipped from his consciousness. Now for the rest of the story:

> I had been the senior pastor for twenty-eight years when we decided
> to do the experiment using the discipleship strategy laid out in this
> book, *Transforming Discipleship*. In the first year we launched four
> groups: three quads and one triad for a total of fifteen people. This

was done purely under the radar. The four of us on staff told no one what was going on. But within a few weeks we all sensed the growth and excitement in our hearts knowing God was at work. Toward the end of the year the groups began to multiply. This is when we began to suspect that we started something extraordinary. At the end of the second year the groups had grown to thirty-six, and at the end of the third year we were up to sixty-four. Not everyone was able to take the lead in establishing their own group immediately, but we could see the process was working. The testimonies of life change, the empowerment of seeing so many taking responsibility for creating the environment in which others could be discipled, infused life into our congregation like I had never seen it before. After five years over four hundred people have been engaged in intentional discipleship to the point where it now defines our congregation. This is who we are and what we are to be about. So excited did we get about what we were seeing that we sensed that we have to export this to others. We have since sponsored two international forums where we have brought people from over fifteen countries to be trained to take back the same approach of intentional disciple making back to their home countries. In thirty-two years of pastoring I have never experienced more church unity and harmony, everybody on the same page, convinced we were doing exactly what Jesus intended his church to do.[10]

Can you see what this careful approach to growing disciples would do for the health of the church or ministry? Can you visualize the impact of multiplication over three to five to seven years? I have watched the effect these multiplying discipleship groups have on a church. Over time the church culture is so transformed that a new consensus develops. People aspire to become self-initiating, reproducing, fully devoted followers of Jesus.

The Hinge

I began chapter six with the image of a hinge. The church, I said, is like a nonfunctioning door because it leans against the biblical doorframe of the call to disciple making. The hinge that connects the door to the doorframe is a practical strategy. The necessary elements in a church-based strategy to make reproducing disciples are to establish a relational disciple-making process that is rooted in a reproducible model (triads or quads) that brings together the transformative elements of life change.

As we turn to chapter nine, we will apply grease to the hinges that keep the door (the church) swinging freely in the door frame (biblical vision): the implementation steps to create a multiplying network of discipleship microgroups.

9

PRACTICALITIES OF
DISCIPLE MAKING

Have you ever had the nagging feeling that there is something in your life you are supposed to do, but you don't have a model or picture in your mind of what to do? We know that we are to leave a legacy of changed lives. Yet it remains an unattainable ideal because we don't have a practical strategy to make it a reality. We want to be able to say what Paul said about those who came after him, "You yourselves are our letter, written on our hearts, to be known and read by all; and you show that you are a letter of Christ, prepared by us, written not with ink but with the Spirit of the living God, not on tablets of stone but on tablets of human hearts" (2 Corinthians 3:2-3). I continue to be moved by the phrase in the letter from Jane (p. 129), who wrote, "I feel like I am the fruit of your fruit! And praise the Lord more fruit is being produced!" I know that this is the only thing that matters. How do we go about seeing the creation of living epistles in the form of self-initiating, reproducing, fully devoted followers of Jesus?

My hope is that through this book you have been given a means to leave a legacy. For many it is not a matter of motivation but know-how. We lack a working model of how to take the approach of Jesus and Paul and make it a reality in ministry and church life. In this chapter I intend to be as practical as possible and leave little to the imagination.

Our agenda in this chapter is to address the following practical questions:

- What is a workable disciple-making model?

- Who should we invite into the discipling process?

- How do we get started?
- How can we grow a multigenerational network of disciples?
- How do we keep up the motivation for multiplication through the generations?

A Workable Disciple-Making Model

When I was in college, Corrie ten Boom, the great Dutch Christian and survivor of Nazi German prison camps, spoke to our group. I don't have a clear recollection of the question I asked her, but I do remember her response. I suppose I was trying to impress my peers with some profound query. She stopped me in my tracks. "K.I.S.S.," she said. "Keep it simple, stupid." What I propose may sound insultingly simple. Yet it has been my experience that if our ministry schemes are overly complex, either they will never get off the ground or will eventually collapse under their own administrative weight.

Here is how it works: Invest in a relationship with two or three others for a year, give or take. Meet weekly for approximately ninety minutes. (A discipling relationship varies in length because of the relational dynamics and the growth processes unique to each relationship.) Then multiply. Each person invites two or three others for the next leg of the journey and does it all again. Same content, different relationships. People have asked me, "Won't this get boring covering the same content repeatedly?" My standard reply from experience is a resounding *no*! Why? The relational dynamics are always different, and this difference keeps the process interesting. People are wonderfully unique. Each microgroup will have its own life or personality because the people, who are different, will make it stimulating. If you are the initiator of the discipling relationship, you also will have grown and be at another stage of development. Let the network grow organically. Multiplication begets multiplication. And in three to five to seven years, you will look back at the family tree and see that the branches have stretched to five or six generations. Joy will come when you see names of people in the family, three or four generations removed from you, that can be traced back to your initial microgroup (see fig. 9.1).

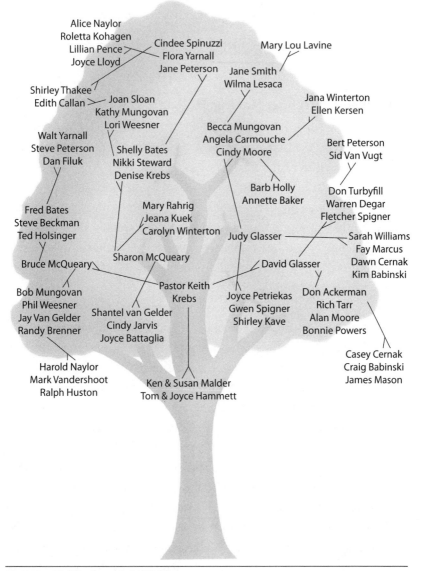

Figure 9.1. The "family tree" of a discipler

Who Is Invited?

You are ready to take the plunge and experiment with a discipleship microgroup. But how do you discern whom you should approach? Remember that a distinguishing dynamic of a discipling relationship that varies from other mentoring relationships is that the discipler issues the call.[1] Just as Jesus was drawn to and named those who would be a part of his inner circle, so we go to people God places on our heart and ask them to join us on the journey of becoming a disciple. This means that the invitation to discipleship should be preceded by a period of prayerful discernment. It is vital to have a settled conviction that the Lord is drawing us to those we are issuing this invitation to.

What criteria should we use to guide our prayer for those who would join us on the discipleship journey? We should look for the same qualities in people that Jesus spotted in the Twelve or that Paul urged Timothy to observe when entrusting the gospel to the next generation: faithfulness, reliability or dependability (2 Timothy 2:2).

Jesus did not seem to be in a hurry to name the Twelve. Perhaps six to nine months transpired from the commencement of his public ministry until he publicly identified those who would be his apostles. His selection of the Twelve followed a night in prayer. His entire ministry rested on the quality of people he chose. If you are going to invest a year or more of your time with two to three others with the intent of multiplying, the people you invite is of paramount importance. When I assumed my role as executive pastor of discipleship in October 2002 at Christ Church of Oak Brook (Illinois), I didn't start my first microgroup until April 2003. Since we were strategically launching this new initiative that we hoped would transform a church, those I chose to be on the ground floor was critical. I eventually invited three members of our board of trustees because I observed hungry hearts; in addition they were strategically positioned to be culture shapers. One of them frankly admitted to me that he had held organization positions for so long that his soul was shriveling. He was a dry sponge ready to soak up refreshing waters.

What were the qualities Jesus looked for in those he called, and how do these qualities serve as a guide for us? I would propose two primary qualities as determinative: loyalty and teachability.

Loyalty. Jesus had a wonderful sense of humor. The day Jesus made Peter the most successful fisherman he had ever been was the day Jesus called him away from his trade. After Peter had been fishing all night, having caught nothing and having cleaned and hung up his nets to dry,

Jesus asked him to go fishing again. With reluctance, while probably muttering under his breath something like, "What does a rabbi know about fishing?" Peter dropped his net into the sea, only to haul in the largest catch of his life. No fish story Peter had ever heard or told came close to this incident. Against this backdrop of smashing triumph, Jesus said to Peter and the others, "From now on you will be catching people" (Luke 5:10). Peter and the others left their means of support, families and familiar surroundings to meander from village to village, following this renegade carpenter. Jesus sought in his followers loyalty to him above all else.

Though we may not be called away from our places of employment and families on an itinerant, apostolic ministry, Jesus still seeks followers who value him above all else. This is evidenced by a willingness to align our behavior and lifestyle with Jesus' desires, an openness to self-examination and a hunger to place our lives at his disposal. Our prayer might be, "Lord, give me eyes to see, and draw my heart to those who have a deep desire to be all you want them to be. May that be true of me also."

Teachability. Jesus chose the disciples for who they would become, not for who they were at the time of their call. We noted in chapter four that the disciples seemed to have no distinguishing characteristics according to the world's standards. None held key positions of influence. They were not drawn from the respected religious ranks, such as the Levitical priesthood or the religious Supreme Court, the Sanhedrin. They had not acquired the equivalent of a PhD, which would give them academic credentials. They fit Paul's description of the Corinthians: "Not many of you were wise by human standards, not many were powerful, not many were of noble birth" (1 Corinthians 1:26).

This should serve as a caution. There is a temptation to base our selection on what might distinguish people according to cultural norms. Leaders in the church are often selected because of natural leadership ability, an outgoing personality, membership in a respected profession, reputation, or positions of influence or wealth. Jesus' thought was *Give me teachable, loyal people, and watch me change the world.* There is almost the sense that the less a person has invested in the world, the more available he or she would be to Jesus. We can easily overlook a disciple who has great potential because he or she does not match the world's value system.

In my first professional ministry with college students, the quiet, shy and unremarkable often became the most focused, influential disciples of Jesus by the time they became juniors and seniors. In Jane Smith's letter to me eight years after her graduation from the University of Pittsburgh, she referred to three students who were most influential in her life. I had the privilege of close association with the two men and one woman. When they arrived as freshmen at the university, they were naturally reticent and, by personality, not standouts. Yet they desired to follow the adventurous life Jesus called them to. They grew into self-initiating, reproducing followers of Jesus.[2] By contrast, the most self-assured, outgoing, attractive person may not be willing to pay the price of discipleship. Though it is tempting to place the charismatic *personalities* front and center and though they may receive the accolades of the crowd, behind the scenes they might not be willing to discipline themselves as leaders.

It's remarkable that Jesus turned the world upside down with fishermen, a tax collector and a terrorist (religious zealot). Never underestimate what can be done with loyal and teachable people. Teachability is a hunger to learn and the humility to not care who you learn it from.

In one of my triads there was a man in his early thirties. I was drawn to him because of his evident desire to know what God had designed him to do with his life. He was reading books on how to get in touch with the passions that God had placed in his heart. He made appointments with people he thought could help him discern his spiritual gift and aid in the discovery of his call. He worked as an engineer designing air conditioning systems. But he was drawn to children and wondered if he should be a teacher. He volunteered one night a week as a counselor with a program called Confident Kids and took one morning a week to act as an aide in a kindergarten classroom to explore whether this was God's call on his life. He is a poster child for teachability.

Admittedly, the process of discerning who God is drawing you to is not an exact science. I resonate with Randy Pope's assessment of the way he finds candidates for his discipleship groups. "I'll share with you my own pattern.... You may find it frustratingly vague, but it's been quite reliable."[3] It is vague because discernment relies on the subjective inner conviction of the Holy Spirit as you sense loyalty and teachability. There are even times when the Spirit leads against all evidence. I was praying about the next microgroup I was ready to form. The name of a man kept coming to me, though I had no recent evidence that his heart had changed. I got to know him because he was our estate planning attorney. Bill attended our church with his wife, but she was the one with the heart for God. Bill was off to the golf course as soon as he appeased his wife by fulfilling his worship obligation. Yet I kept having this nagging sense that I should pursue him. I gave Bill a call and asked if I could meet him at this law office; I had a question I wanted to ask him. I said to him, "I am starting this new group, and I just have this sense I am supposed to ask you to be a part of it." Bill response stunned me. He said, "If you had come to me six months ago I would have turned you down flat. But I was given the book *The Case for Christ* by Lee Strobel. I read it and was stunned by the evidence for the resurrection. Jesus is now intriguing to me. I'd love to be a part of this group." Though I didn't know that Bill's heart had changed, the Lord did. If I had remained with what I knew about Bill, he would not have fit the criteria.

The first step in creating a reproducible discipleship group is to find the right people. The right people are marked by a willingness to be loyal to Jesus and have a teachable spirit. Simply ask the Lord to lay on your heart those he is already working on. Keep a journal. Write down the names of people the Lord seems to bring to mind. Continue to pray over them until there is a settled conviction that the Holy Spirit is tying your lives together.

How to Start

The following step-by-step guide can serve as a blueprint to follow when you are ready to approach people with the invitation to discipleship.

Step 1: Make the invitation. State that as a result of prayer you feel drawn to invite the person to join you in a mutual journey of discipleship toward maturity in Christ. Stress that this is not a random invitation but comes as the fruit of prayer. It might be helpful to express that Jesus' model of making disciples was to have a few who were "with him" and that the way the Lord continues to make disciples is through intentional relationships. If *Discipleship Essentials* is your curriculum of choice, then it would be appropriate to look at its definition of *discipling* on page 17, so that the person has an idea of the kind of relationship this will be.

Step 2: Review the discipleship curriculum. Walk through the table of contents and the layout of one of the lessons so that the disciple gets a sense for what is involved. I would also stress the fact that discipling is not about completing a lesson in a workbook. The curriculum is a tool that provides some structure for the relationship. Tools do not make disciples. The Lord uses people to make disciples. The tool raises the issues of discipleship, but the discipler incarnates the principles and convictions in a life.

Step 3: Review the covenant line by line. Review "A Disciple's Covenant" from page 14 of *Discipleship Essentials* (or whatever covenant you may be using as a basis for accountability). It is imperative that the disciple has the opportunity to ponder the extent of commitment involved in the relationship. This has to do with time expectations (approximately four hours a week of preparation and meeting time, and whatever travel is involved with getting to the meeting place), relational risk and life change. You want to raise the question implicitly: Are you ready to consider serious change in every area of your life? Ask them to restate in their own words what their understanding is of the commitment they are making. From the outset you are raising the bar and calling a person to step up to it.

Step 4: Ask the person to prayerfully consider this relationship over the next week. Do not seek or allow an immediate response to the invitation to join a microgroup. You want the person to consider the time commitment in light of the larger configuration of life's responsibilities and to make the adjustments in their schedule, if necessary, to make this relationship work. I often ask them to consider things they might have to delete from their weekly schedules in order to make room for this commitment. Many people live right up the margins of their life and simply cannot add anything more. In addition, you want a person to ruminate over internal readiness, which usually means facing the fear of what might be ahead. I would be very concerned if a potential disciple did not have some fear or concern about keeping the commitment. You want the weight of the commitment to be felt.

Step 5: Inform the person that a third or fourth person will be joining you in the microgroup. If you have not settled on or do not already have a third or fourth person in mind, enlist this person's support in helping discern who that person (or persons) should be.

Step 6: Set the meeting time of your first gathering. At the first meeting of the discipleship group, ask each person, yourself included, to share the process he or she went through in making the commitment to this group. Were there any adjustments to their schedules that had to be made? Were there inner impediments that had to be faced? Go back through the covenant as a group, again asking their understanding of what they think they are committing to. I like to have a covenant signing ceremony at the first meeting. In each other's presence each person signs the covenant as an open demonstration of everyone's commitment to keep the covenant and as an invitation to be held accountable to it by each other. Note that there will be a couple of opportunities to review and renew the covenant in *Discipleship Essentials* (pp. 80, 146). These are times for self-evaluation against the covenantal standards, as well as chances to reflect on your level of satisfaction with the microgroup experience to date. Each person enters with specific expectations as to what they think the relationship will be. It is important for each to be able to share disappointments, if there have been any, and make course corrections. The time of review also serves as an opportunity to celebrate the benefits while in the process as well. It is important that the invitees know that a major role of the convener is to be a keeper of the covenant. The leader is there to help the members complete what they say they are committed to accomplish.

Step 7: Guide the participants through the sessions. In an hour and a half session I would allow about thirty minutes for personal sharing, follow-up from previous sessions, mutual enjoyment of what is happening in each other's lives, and prayer. The other hour is spent on the responses to the questions in the material that each person has previously prepared. Go at a pace that seems comfortable to the group, and don't be so regimented that you do not allow time to chase rabbit trails. You want to encourage participants to introduce questions that are prompted from the study. It is also important not to rush the personal application to the various dimensions of life. In *Discipleship Essentials* questions have been carefully crafted to bring the truth home to the lives of discipleship partners. There will be times when the personal issues people are facing are so tantamount that you will set aside any normal agenda to stay with the challenge in their life.

Step 8: The convener of the triad completes all the lessons and models initial leadership. The convener also fully participates in the discussions with his or her insights as one of the participating members of the group. For the first six sessions together the convener will serve as the model of how to use the time together and cover the discipleship content. Yet the format is so simple that leadership is easily transferable. After these initial sessions encourage a rotation of leadership. The primary role of the leader is to guide the opening sharing and walk the group through the lesson material that is already laid out. Rotating leadership of the sessions has the value in allowing each person early on to gain the confidence that he or she could lead such a group in the future.

Step 9: The discipler models transparency. The group will probably go as deep personally as, or take risks to the extent that, they see the leader doing. This discipler shares his or her own personal struggles, prayer concerns and confession of sin. But trust develops incrementally. The degree of self-revelation will need to be matched to the level of trust that has been developed. In addition, the disciplers need not feel that they have all the answers to the biblical and theological questions raised. Feel free to say, "I don't know, but I will find out" or "Why don't we each seek answers to that question this week and come back to share our insights?" Discipleship is, in part, about taking responsibility and initiative to search out the truth.

Growing a Multigenerational Network of Disciples

We now move from the focus on a single microgroup to the fulfillment of a vision that there will be a multiplication of self-initiating, reproducing followers of Jesus. We visualize cell reproduction, where the DNA from an initial cell replicates itself in adjoining cells (see fig. 9.2). How do we lay the foundations for this kind of reproduction?

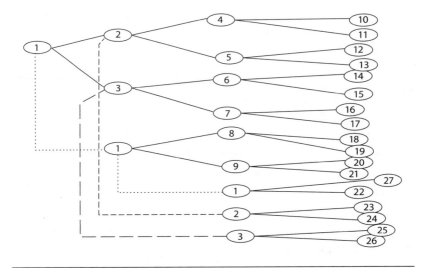

Figure 9.2. Multiplication

Almost everything I say in this section will put the brakes on our attempt to speed up the process of replication.

Start with one triad. My advice to those who are just starting to experience the dynamics of this type of discipleship relationship is to take a year and "just do it" (my apologies to Nike). Get a feel for what happens in a small discipleship group. Place the discipling partners high on your prayer list. Make regular intercession for them based on the identified areas of needed growth. In addition, ask the Lord to show you what your disciples could become under his shaping influence. Just as Jesus saw that Peter would be "the rock" when he was anything but, so ask the Lord to ignite your imagination to see the potential purpose and call that the Lord has on these lives.

If you are using a curriculum like *Discipleship Essentials*, it is helpful to master its content so you have a lifetime discipleship tool at your disposal. Having gone through various versions of *Discipleship Essentials* over the last thirty years, I can almost tell you what is on each page of the material. I have found it enormously valuable to have this tucked away in my head and heart, because it serves as a resource to inform my teaching, fuel any counsel I give and provide a filter to screen the world's messages.

Let me for a moment speak particularly to pastors or Christian leaders whose professional role it is to pass on "the good deposit of the gospel." I have for a long time felt that we are an underutilized resource because we generally have not had the means to pass on the content of our theological training through the filter of our life experience. By mastering a discipleship tool, we give ourselves a theological grid through which to pass our storehouse of knowledge. A discipleship group provides us the incentive and context to tuck away in our own hearts "the good treasure entrusted to you" (2 Timothy 1:14).

A multigenerational network of discipleship may seem to have meager beginnings if it starts with one discipleship microgroup. But you have to begin somewhere and get beyond the need to have a big splash that will lead to instantaneous change. Quick fixes have led to the discipleship morass we are in. Even though the need for discipling will run way ahead of your ability to meet it in the short run, remember that programs have failed to deliver the necessary life change over time. A generation ago Leroy Eims asked, "What then is the problem today? Why don't we see more of this [disciple making] going on? Why are fruitful, dedicated mature disciples so rare? The biggest reason is that all too often we have relied on programs or materials or some other thing to do the job. The ministry is carried on by people, not programs."[4]

Have a long-term vision. Jesus went about his ministry with a relaxed urgency. He never seemed to be in a hurry but always kept his eye laser focused on the destination. Jesus had a conscious awareness that he was a man born to die. Always looming ahead was his rendezvous with self-sacrifice. It was for "this hour" that he had come. Yet along the way he was training his disciples to carry on after he left. Jesus knew that the disciples' training program would terminate with the completion of his mission in the cross. It would be their turn to carry on the mission. The baton had to be passed. Jesus never wavered from that vision.

How long do you have left in your present ministry? Will you be there three years, five years, seven years or longer? What do you want to leave behind? There is a saying in relationship to change: You never seem to accomplish as much as you want in the short run but can accomplish a lot more than you can imagine in the long run. Start building a network of disciple making. Fight every impulse in your being that says, "We must see results by next month (or even in the next six months)." Intentionally growing people takes time. You can't accomplish as much as you like in the short run, but you will be able to see far more than you can imagine in the long run.

One of the mistakes I was graciously rescued from, which taught me hard lessons, had to do with trying to rapidly multiply disciples. (Any time you hear people say that they have an approach to rapidly grow disciples, treat them as if they are used car salesmen. If anything sounds too good to be true, it probably is.) In my first experiment with these microgroups, I had started and developed the network exclusively among men, since I was the initiator of this ministry. Once the replication had occurred through a few triads, women in the congregation began clamoring for something similar. I had a brainstorm. I decided to issue an invitation to approximately fifteen highly regarded, spiritually mature women to come to a Saturday morning session where I would lay out for them the challenge and vision of disciple making. The Saturday morning arrived. I was deeply gratified that these quality people would take the time to hear the challenge I was to place before them. I gave what I thought was one of my best "win one for the Gipper" speeches. In order to provide the biblical imperative, I sketched out Jesus' approach to investing in a few. I affirmed that others in the congregation looked up to them as winsome followers of Jesus. The time for the "ask" had come. "I challenge you to find two other women who could join you in a journey of discipleship. You be their guides into deeper maturity in Christ so that we can develop this discipling network among women in our congregation as well."

Expecting that these women would storm the locker room door in order to take their places on the playing field, I was thoroughly deflated by their response. "Coach," they said, "we hate to tell you, but before we can play the game, we need to know the fundamentals. We have never experienced the kind of relationship you are describing. How can you expect us to lead people through something that we have never experienced? Why don't you slow down? Instead, you take two of us through what you have in mind. Lay a solid foundations for their lives and build from there." I was trying to jump-start discipling among the women. I wanted to launch fifteen groups simultaneously. *A perfect plan to rapidly grow disciples,* I thought. I guess I was the used car salesman that day. I had visions of a transformed congregation within two years. They said, essentially, "Take a long-term view. Slow down. Do it right." And they were right.

A growing discipleship network is like yeast slowly penetrating the dough, causing it to rise almost imperceptibly. In the first year of an initial triad, we have the satisfaction of watching intimacy develop and transformation occur. In the second year we encourage and coach two new triads into existence, and start a third one of our own. In the third year, these three have become nine, and so on. It takes up to five years before critical mass has been reached. As I said before, it takes less than 20 percent of a congregation to set the pace for the rest. A small percentage of value holders determine what a church or ministry is all about. At the five-year mark there are so many stories of life change, and so much buzz about what these triads have meant to those involved, that people will beg for the opportunity to become a part of these groups.

I can hear it now. "Five years! I don't have five years!" Are you going to be there five years from now? Then what do you want to leave behind? If you are a pastor reading this book, do you want to measure your ministry by the number of sermons preached, worship services designed, homes visited, hospital calls made, counseling sessions held, or the number of self-initiating, reproducing, fully devoted followers of Jesus? I reiterate, the church is in its present predicament because we do not have enough leaders who have the vision to think small.

Let me remind you of Robert Coleman's challenge: "One must decide where he wants his ministry to count—in the momentary applause of popular recognition or in the reproduction of his life in a few chosen ones who will carry on his work after he has gone? Really, it is a question of which generation we are living for."[5]

Select carefully and wisely. The key element in growing a multi-generational network of disciple making is to start with the right people. Just as a building is only as strong as its foundation, so those you select to initiate the network will determine whether multiplication occurs.

Your initial selection will vary depending on your discipling model and context of ministry. The primary setting I have had in mind throughout this book is the myriad of established churches with little to no intentional disciple making. If this describes your situation, I would begin with the most well-grounded and respected followers of Jesus in your community. In addition, they should be stable members of your community. In other words, look for people who have a good chance of staying around for a while.

Why should you begin with those who already appear to be fairly mature in the faith? First, they probably have not been discipled or taught to disciple others. The group of women I met with were highly regarded for their spiritual depth, but to a person they had never been intentionally discipled nor discipled others. You have a great opportunity to take those who have already demonstrated a heart for God and turn them into reproducers. Second, their reputations, for all the right reasons, will give credibility to this new discipling adventure. Third, you want to ensure, as much as you can, a return on your investment. When you spend approximately a year with two or three others, you want to know that this was worthwhile. You are trying to see people become self-initiating followers of Jesus, and you also want them to adopt a lifestyle of reproduction. You are growing disciple makers. Those who are well grounded and stable, who have already demonstrated that they are dependable, reliable and faithful, are your best bet for replication.

The previous paragraph was written primarily for those who are attempting to lead a church through renewal. For those who are in a setting where more people are coming to Christ than you can keep up with, you have another challenge. You cannot wait five years; you will be committing spiritual infanticide if you do. In this setting you must take a two-pronged approach. You need to gather people in small groups (of approximately ten) for fellowship and provide them with some spiritual grounding. It is much easier and quicker to grow small-group leaders who can create at the least a minimal nurturing environment. At the same time you must begin to do all that I said previously in regard to discipling and let the network grow. In five to seven years you will have produced enough disciplers for all the new converts, but in the meantime you must settle for larger nurturing fellowship groups.

What if you are planting a church? This is the perfect time to make disciple making a part of the lifestyle of the congregation. A part of every staff person's job description is to have at least two others they are investing in.

For an alternative discipling model, I commend to you Neil Cole's *Life Transformation Groups*.[6] Cole focuses on a different target group. He uses these LTGs, as he calls them, as an evangelistic tool. His heart is to witness transformation in the lives of the most unlikely unbelievers. His LTGs meet in coffeehouses where the tattooed, body pierced and purple haired may be found. The future leaders in his ministry have been called out of lifestyles in open rebellion against God to a transformed life in Jesus Christ.

Under this heading of selecting carefully and wisely, it is appropriate to identify my failings. The mistakes I have made have usually occurred when others have approached me and asked if I would disciple them or if they could be in one of my microgroups. Why might this be grounds for caution? First, it is very flattering to have people want to spend time with you. Second, it is hard to displease people. How do you say no to people who want to grow in Christ? For these two reasons, it is difficult to pray with objectivity about whether this person is God's call on your time. Since a necessary characteristic of disciple making is for the discipler to issue the call, in this situation the discipler is being asked to confirm someone else's request. But this is not the most serious reservation. Not only are your motives in question, but so are the motives of the one who has approached you. What is the person's reason for requesting to be in a microgroup with you?

My two most disappointing microgroup experiences came as a result of responding to the requests of others while not carefully examining the reasons they wanted to be with me. Here is the real issue. What is the motive for wanting to be in a discipling relationship? Is it primarily to grow into Christlikeness, or is there a hidden agenda?

In the first instance, I, a new pastor at the church, was approached by two men who wanted to provide support for me while I was getting my legs in this new ministry. I was flattered and certainly in need. What was intended to be a support for me and a discipleship group for the three of us quickly became neither. From all that I could tell, these men appeared to be highly motivated disciples of Jesus. One had spent a number of years in a church-planting ministry in Europe, while the other had a reputation for entrepreneurial ministry as a businessman. I didn't discern that these two were disgruntled ex-elders who had moved to the margin of the church. Week after week I was bombarded with a litany of complaints about the current group of elders, the self-focused nature of the church, the style of worship, the lack of evangelism and so on. After some months I told them that their negative attitude was detrimental to my ability to lead the church that I was learning to love.

The second aborted experience also included a person who wanted to spend some time with me. Sam was an outgoing and brash owner of his own small business. He and his family were high profile and deeply invested in the church's ministry. Their children were scattered throughout the youth program, and Sam's wife was the "mother" to half of the teenagers in the congregation (or so it seemed). Sam was a salesman par excellence, and he sold me on his eagerness for this type of relationship. Problems began to show up early on. Sam would come to our sessions with the weekly assignment only partially completed. He sometimes arrived late or had some reason to leave early. It was evident he was not ready for this discipline, because ultimately he was not serious about integrating all of his life under the lordship of Christ.

A confrontation with Sam was precipitated after people from the congregation stated to me their surprise that he was a part of a discipleship group. These people were employees in Sam's business. In the workplace Sam's demeanor was different from the warm persona he displayed in the church community. According to them, he was a tyrant. His emotional outbursts caused everyone to walk on eggshells. I eventually had to ask Sam about the accuracy of this inconsistency between his church face and the face he presented elsewhere. A person who truly wanted to be a disciple of Jesus would have responded—if not initially, then eventually—in a spirit of repentance. He would have acknowledged his double life as contrary to Christ's desires and asked the group to help him live a consistent life for Christ's sake. Instead, he cut off the relationship because he was offended that I would raise such an issue.

Is there any sure way to know the heart of the person you are inviting to join you on this journey? None that I know of. But be appropriately cautious with those who seek to spend time with you. If you are a pastor or a prominent figure in the Christian community, you already know that people might vicariously gain a sense of self-importance through association. This is not the fertile soil out of which a disciple is made.

If you want to grow a multigenerational discipling network, start with one microgroup, have a long-term vision, and select carefully and wisely, especially at the foundational stage of establishing the network.

Keeping the Motivation for Multiplication

Once the discipling network begins to multiply, a concern will naturally arise. How do you keep putting energy into the system once it moves away from the center of vision? To start anything of significance there must be a visionary who is energized to see it become a reality. This is true of discipling. The visionary sees the possibilities of a multigenerational disciple-making network. He or she is committed to making self-initiating, reproducing disciples of Jesus as a lifestyle, but once the initial groups have given birth, can the vision for reproduction be sustained? In other words, how do you pastor a decentralized ministry?

One of the temptations to avoid is to solve this problem by turning discipling into a program and thereby killing this self-reproducing organism. In my pastorates we never made a public recruiting announcement about this discipleship ministry. Come September, when all church ministries resume, we didn't make a Sunday morning announcement about the opportunity to be in a discipleship group. We avoided putting the groups onto a synchronized schedule following the school calendar from September to June. Occasionally we might have participants share the life-changing benefits with the congregation in worship, retreats or other ministries. Even after the public witness we didn't give people a ready-made way to get into a discipleship group. I wanted the hunger and intrigue to build. I avoided making this ministry into a program we had to sustain by building an administrative superstructure. The genius behind microgroups is that we can start them without having to run a gauntlet of committees and thereby having the idea talked to death by people who do not have a heart for what we are trying to accomplish. To sustain the network we need only a small oversight group to sustain the practice and vision of multiplication.

What does this oversight group do to sustain the vision and energy for multiplication? The following were some of the varied ways we experimented with energy infusion.

Periodically call together the discipling network as a whole for sharing, motivation and instruction. Occasionally we invited all the current participants in the microgroups together to cross-pollinate. Since an individual group can feel isolated and disconnected, we were constantly looking for ways to help people feel a part of a movement. At these gatherings we would mix up the participants to form sharing groups. People would share with each other their reasons for responding to the invitation and the particular flavor of their group life. We would handpick two or three people to tell about the influence this experience had on their lives. An exhortation would be issued from Scripture to carry on the discipling chain to the next generation.

Invite a guest speaker. A variation is to invite a speaker who is committed to disciple making and can speak with passion. One highlight was the privilege of having Keith Phillips from World Impact address our burgeoning network. He had written *The Making of a Disciple* and had fully integrated a disciple-making strategy into the urban centers of the United States. Having an outside voice reinforce what you have been saying raises your credibility. A guest can say things in a fresh way, using life-impacting stories from their context to reignite the vision of multiplication.

Meet with discipling leaders in groups of three or four. In between the larger group motivational settings, it is fruitful to bring together three or four microgroup conveners to process their experience together. One of the roles of those in your discipling oversight group could be to convene these smaller sessions. We found it invaluable for the leaders of the groups to share mutual experiences, problem solve and gain ideas from each other as to how they were handling their time in their groups. This then became another opportunity to remind them to challenge their group members to reproduce.

Meet with those in the last third of their triad. Depending on how thorough you want to be in knowing where the groups are on their discipleship journey, you might want to meet with those who are beyond the two-thirds mark in completing their discipleship curriculum. *Discipleship Essentials* has a trigger point built into the curriculum where the participants are to begin praying about and selecting those who will join them in the next leg of the journey. If you know groups who are approaching this point, a contact can be made to encourage them to follow this process. It is also helpful to know if and why people are reticent to reproduce.

Publish a discipleship newsletter. I would encourage you to create an electronic publication that is sent out on a regular basis to all those in the discipling network. In previous churches I have served, one newsletter was *Discipling Network News* (Southern California) and another called *Discipleship Bytes* (Silicon Valley). The Camarillo Community Church calls their publication *Discipleship Essentials*. The purpose of the newsletter is primarily to help people feel that they are a part of a growing organism. Written testimonies of group participants serve to encourage others. Articles on the biblical vision of discipling are a way to keep connecting people back to the initial impetus. Names are listed of all microgroup participants to create the feel that God is up to something big.

In my experience this approach to disciple making has yielded approximately a two-thirds reproduction rate for at least one generation following the initial completion of a microgroup. Pressing responsibilities in a given week can take a pastor far afield from the people-building business. No matter how crazy my week became, I knew that I had at least one opportunity in my weekly schedule to feel like I was fulfilling my pastoral call to make disciples of all nations.

Leaving a Legacy

One of the most deflating moments for the United States' Olympic team occurred in 1988 in Seoul, Korea. The American 4x100 relay team was poised to break the world record and assume its position as the best in the world. It had peerless athletes. There was no thought that this team could lose. The only question was whether they would crack the world record. Yet as the final leg of the race approached, the unthinkable happened. The Americans dropped the baton. The handoff was not completed. In an instant, the race was over. The crowd, electrified moments earlier, were left in stunned silence. The American team had arrogantly relied on their inherent speed and failed to sufficiently practice the handoff, which is so crucial for the completion of the race.

"Every Christian must look on himself as a link between two generations," writes William Barclay.[7] We need to practice the handoff. When all else fails, read the directions. It is not that Jesus' way has been tried and found wanting; it has been largely talked about but not implemented. Return to small, reproducible, long-term relationships as the means of transmission of the gospel from one generation to the next.

Legacies are not about leaving large sums of money to our children or being immortalized by getting our names etched on a building. When we get to the shore's edge and know that there is a boat there waiting to take us to the other side to be with Jesus, all that will truly matter is the names of family, friends and others who are self-initiating, reproducing, fully devoted followers of Jesus because we made it the priority of our lives to walk with them toward maturity in Christ. There is no better eternal investment or legacy to leave behind.

This sentiment is captured well in "The Bridge Builder," a poem by Will Allen Dromgoole.

> An old man, going a lone highway,
> Came at evening, cold and gray,
> To a chasm, vast and deep and wide,
> Through which was flowing a sullen tide.
> The old man crossed the twilight dim—
> That sullen stream had no fears for him;
> But he turned, when he had reached the other side,
> He built a bridge to span the tide.
>
> "Old man," said a fellow pilgrim near,
> "You are wasting strength building here.
> Your journey will end with the ending day;

You never again will pass this way.
You have crossed the chasm, deep and wide,
Why build up the bridge at the eventide?"

The builder lifted his old gray head.
"Good friend, in the path I have come," he said,
"There followeth after me today
A youth whose feet must pass this way.
This chasm that has been naught to me
To that fair-haired youth may be a pitfall be.
He, too, must cross in the twilight dim;
Good friend, I am building the bridge for him."[8]

10

The Role of Preaching in Making Disciples

You might be asking yourself, *If disciple making is fundamentally a relational process, what is the role of preaching in making reproducing disciples of Jesus?* Or, *What are the contributions and limitations of preaching in making disciples of Jesus?*

Let me start provocatively: if we could make disciples by preaching to people, the job would have been done a long time ago. This may seem like a strange way to introduce the topic of the role of preaching in making disciples. Yet I assert this from the outset to highlight how much weight and freight we put on preaching as the central event in the church.

Let's acknowledge the place that preaching generally has in the life of most congregations. The following are signs of the importance we place on preaching.

1. When a church is looking for a new pastor, what is the number one item on people's minds? The quality and power of the pastor's preaching. We ask of the prospective pastor, "Please send a CD of your sermons. Is there a website that features videos of your preaching?" If the person cannot pass muster at this point, he or she is eliminated from further consideration.

What is a search committee saying by placing preaching at the top of the list? Way down in order of importance is the quality of their love for the flock, their emotional maturity, their model of personal disciple making and so forth. None of this matters if the person cannot preach to the standard desired.

2. What is the proposed first solution to address a deficit identified in the church? When we are trapped in the 80-20 rule of stewardship, where 20 percent give 80 percent to the church finances, what is the suggested first step? The stewardship committee will propose to the pastor that he or she do a series of sermons on tithing. When it is observed that people are not bringing the right spirit to worship, insert the magic bullet and preach a series of sermons on the heart of true worship. Preaching is the first step in addressing a particular lack in Christian living. This may seem like a caricature, but in my experience it is not too far off-track.

The Limitations of Preaching

So from the outset let's acknowledge the limitations of preaching when it comes to making disciples, or why it takes more than preaching to make disciples.

1. Preaching requires little from the listener. Good preaching requires considerable effort on the part of the preacher but very little from the person in the pew. There is nothing more demanding for a pastor than preparing quality, biblical teaching on a weekly basis. People come to worship expecting that a Scripture text has been mined for its meaning; woven in are relevant life illustrations or compelling stories complete with some practical suggestions on how to apply the message to one's life. It's entirely different for the person in the pew, who can be positively or negatively inclined toward the sermon without ever having to tip his or her hand. After the service people shake the preacher's hand and offer some response: "Thanks, pastor, that really spoke to me this morning!" or perhaps, "That was the best sermon on that subject I have ever heard!" The last comment might keep the preacher going for another month. Yet the parishioners are not accountable to actually incorporate what they heard.

2. Preaching is often unprocessed. Preaching often does not come with a context to engage what has been heard. In what setting does the listener wrestle with the preached word so that it personally is applied as God's Word for their life? After the sermon most worship services conclude with a prayer and closing hymn, and perhaps a benediction. We are not invited to sit quietly before the Word, asking the Lord to have his truth penetrate our being through the Holy Spirit's work. Much would be added to the gravity of the preached word if we paused for a moment of quiet reflection, noting a point of truth or two that penetrated our life. Most of us don't have a community of people who ask each other, "What did you hear today? What was the truth or word from God that spoke to you?" Rarely do we have the opportunity to hear how others are taking in the truth and applying it to their lives. What happens to the state of our hearts if week in and week out we listen to messages with unprocessed content?

Of my thirty-eight years in professional ministry, I've had one five-year stint out of the pastorate with a role in an educational institution. During this time I was primarily a person in the pew rather than the preacher. I got the view from the pew as an ordinary member of a congregation. It was eye-opening for me. Here was my bottom-line observation: Unprocessed preaching can be toxic to one's spirit, or at the very least it can create a resistance or hardening. Unless we have a way to stay with and absorb the preached word, we can too easily close our hearts to its impact.

3. Preaching can be information download. In the evangelical world the Word is central. Some church traditions believe that expositional preaching through books of the Bible is all that is needed for transformation. In other words, we tend to equate information with transformation. This is not to underestimate the power of the preached word, but simply to acknowledge its limitations as a standalone event. I affirm the value of teaching for the body of Christ, but we should recognize that the worship experience can be turned into a classroom where we take copious notes. To the extent that this ends with privatized application, we have eliminated the "iron sharpens iron" relational component, which is essential for discipleship.

4. Preaching was not Jesus' primary means of making disciples. Not even Jesus believed he could make disciples by teaching them in groups. As we noted in chapter three, though Jesus spoke to crowds, he was appropriately skeptical of people's motivations: "Jesus . . . would not entrust himself to them, because he knew all people and needed no one to testify about anyone; for he himself knew what was in everyone" (John 2:24-25). Jesus staked the future of his ministry on the few that were called to be a part of his inner circle. Jesus could not transfer his character, message and mission en masse. He needed life investment, teachable moments, character-shaping encounters and practice sessions for short-term mission. None of these can be accomplished by addressing an audience. So Jesus chose the means of relational life investment as the way to form disciples.

I have begun this chapter analyzing the focus we put on preaching because of the unrealistic role it plays in most churches. Obviously, throughout this book I have emphasized the need to shift to a relational setting as the formative context to make disciples. However, preaching contributes significantly to the disciple-making environment in the life of a church.

Let me highlight three vital and necessary contributions of preaching to the disciple-making mission of the church.

Preaching Declares the Good News of the Gospel

The gospel rightly proclaimed should yield disciples. And yet there appears to be some defect in our message, because there is considerable confusion as to what we mean by *disciple*. A false distinction, often unspoken, has arisen in our time: that a person can be a Christian without being a disciple.

A woman said to her pastor following worship one Sunday, apparently in response to his challenge to be a disciple, "I just want to be a Christian, I don't want to be a disciple. I like my life the way it is. I believe that Jesus died for my sins, and I will be with him when I die. Why do I have to be a disciple?"[1]

One of the major tasks of preaching is to answer this woman's question. Several assumptions need to be corrected if we are going to make disciples. First, she evidently believes that being a Christian and being a disciple are two different things. She could be one without the other. Second, she has reduced the gospel to two things: (1) Jesus had dealt with her sin through his sacrificial death, and (2) this provided life forever with him. In her mind the gospel has no integral connection with being a disciple. It was all about the benefits she had freely received, which came with no obligation. Third, being a disciple, whatever that meant to her, would disturb her current satisfying way of life. Fourth, her question,

"Why do I have to be a disciple?" seems to convey almost dismissively that she has not and does not need to explore the answer to her own question.

This woman has done us the service of making explicit an implicit assumption that lurks within the Christian community. In the contemporary church, this is the elephant in the room. How did this woman arrive at the conclusion that one can be a Christian without being a disciple? To paraphrase Dallas Willard, she concluded this not in spite of what we have been preaching but precisely because of what we have been preaching.

A nondiscipleship gospel. The popular version of our contemporary gospel is designed to produce Christians, as commonly understood, not disciples. Let's look at the usual terms we have been using to proclaim the good news.

Presently, the good news is largely framed in terms of receiving the benefits that Christ has purchased on the cross. Scot McKnight has demonstrated conclusively in his book *The King Jesus Gospel* that we have come to equate the gospel with the "plan of salvation." It is usually summarized in four points:

- God loves you.
- You messed up.
- Jesus died for you.
- Accept Jesus into your heart.[2]

The deal is sealed with the decision question, "Will you receive Jesus Christ right now and trust him alone for forgiveness of sins and eternal life?" An affirmative response is followed by what we commonly call the sinner's prayer: "Dear Jesus, thank you for making it possible for me to find peace with God! I believe that when you died you were paying the penalty for my sins. I now receive you into my life as my Savior, so I can have forgiveness and never-ending life from God! Thanks for the gift of eternal life."[3]

This is the sum total of being a Christian for many people, which is distinguished from being a disciple. Christians are those who have had their sins forgiven because they have put their trust in Christ's substitutionary work on the cross, which then opens the door to an eternal future with Jesus. This directly leads to the woman's question: Why do I have to be a disciple? Nothing in this benefits package even hints at discipleship as either a natural consequence or a necessity.

A discipleship gospel. The role of preaching in disciple making is to proclaim a gospel that actually leads to discipleship. The false, unbiblical distinction that a person can be a Christian without being a disciple is confronted with the gospel that Jesus proclaimed, which leads directly to discipleship.

What was Jesus' gospel? Is it the same gospel that is so prevalent today? According to Mark, Jesus begins his public ministry with this succinct statement of the gospel. "After John was arrested, Jesus came to Galilee, proclaiming the good news of God, and saying, 'The time is fulfilled, and the kingdom of God has come near; repent, and believe in the good news'" (Mark 1:14-15).

Jesus' message was *the good news.* Like announcing the arrival of a dignitary, Jesus trumpeted the glad tidings of God. Yet, ironically, he was tooting his own horn. He was heralding himself as the one in whom the glad tidings were present.

Mark boils down almost in bullet form the four tenets (ironically) that were at the heart of Jesus' gospel:

- The time is fulfilled.

- The kingdom of God is near.

- Repent.

- Believe the good news.

Each phrase is packed with substance.

The time is fulfilled or has come. In the *Message* Eugene Peterson captures the moment simply, "Time's up!" This phrase conjures up the image of a pregnant woman who is closing in on the end of the nine-month waiting period. The culmination commences with birth pangs. Finally, they are five minutes apart, and she announces to her husband, "It's time! Call the doctor! Let's go." The hour has arrived; the waiting is over.

When Jesus says "the time is fulfilled," he ties the gospel story back to the entire story of Israel and views himself at its completion. The

Greek word Jesus chooses for time is *kairos* as opposed to *chronos*. When we ask, "What time is it?" we are speaking of *chronos*. This is ticktock time. One moment is the same as the next. In contrast, *kairos* is opportunity time, a defining moment whose importance is not to be missed. It is time pregnant with significance because of what has happened on a particular day or moment. Americans celebrate the Fourth of July as Independence Day, marking the birth of a nation. It is *kairos*. July 5 is *chronos*, just another day (unless it is your birthday, of course). *Kairos* says that everything will be different from this day forward.

The kingdom of God is near. What is so earth-shattering, Jesus? "The kingdom of God is at hand or has come among you!" Jesus comes on the scene proclaiming the kingdom of God, and he spends his last moments on earth speaking about the kingdom of God (Acts 1:3). In between there are 122 references to the kingdom of God (or the kingdom of heaven) with over ninety of these being on the lips of Jesus. In other words, the setting for Jesus' gospel is the kingdom of God. Notice how different this is from the *transactional* gospel!

Jesus stirred up popular images when he announced the near presence of the kingdom of God. The Hebrew people were longing for their promised deliverer, the Messiah (*Christos*), who would usher in the kingdom of God. One of the things that marked the difference between the chosen people and all others was their view of history. The Jewish people actually believed history was going somewhere; it had a destination, as opposed to meaningless repetitious cycles (summer, fall, winter, spring; birth, life, death, rebirth) of pagan cultures. The people of Israel believed in a sovereign God who divided time into two major eras: *this age* followed by *the age to come*. *This age* was torn asunder by sin and all its consequences, one of which was a shameful dominance by a foreign oppressor (for example, Rome). But all of this would be supplanted by the in-breaking of *the age to come* (the kingdom of God).

A Messiah king would appear dramatically and establish a glorious age of the eternal reign of God on earth. All sin would be forgiven and expunged. The lion would lie down with the lamb. Swords would be beaten into plowshares. Best of all, the enemies of Israel would be vanquished, and the glory days of King David would be restored *forever*.

When Jesus proclaimed, "The kingdom of God is at hand," you can imagine the surge of hope that pulsated through the veins of the people. Jesus the King is bringing the presence of the kingdom. Jesus is the presence of the kingdom.

They would have been partially right. Jesus the King was among them. But he was bringing in a very different kind of kingdom than was anticipated. From the beginning Jesus indicated that he was not going to be a military leader. Even saying "the kingdom of God is at hand" was deliciously ambiguous about the nature of this kingdom. For *at hand* can simultaneously mean "has arrived" or "is near," or "has come" or "is still to come." Which is it? Both. This is why theologians have spoken of the kingdom of God as "already, but not yet."

We live at a time between the times. The already, but the not yet. Jesus brings with him a kingdom different from the one anticipated. How strangely this king wields his power. Human kingdoms have symbols of power like palaces and armies, yet King Jesus has nowhere to lay his head. Human kings rule over their realm on thrones, while King Jesus is lifted up on a cross.

In other words, the kingdom of God is a *secret* government that transcends geographic and political boundaries. It is truly a kingdom without borders. The interior structure of life in this kingdom is ruled by grace and love. While in the world, our King calls us to be different from the world dominated by strife, tribalism and self-exaltation. Those who follow Jesus must change kingdoms. The apostle Paul wrote that the Father "has rescued us from the power of darkness and transferred us into the kingdom of his beloved Son." Only then do we step into the realm where we experience the benefits of the kingdom—the One "in whom we have redemption, the forgiveness of sins" (Colossians 1:13-14). To partake of the benefits we must change kingdoms or realign our loyalty.

Repent. What is the entryway into the kingdom of God? Jesus says, "Here comes the kingdom of God, *repent* and believe the good news." King Jesus stands in our path and says, "You have a choice to make. I am creating a crisis for you, the crisis of opportunity, because ultimately it is good news." It has been noted that the Chinese character for *crisis* is a combination of danger and opportunity. The danger is, of course, missing the opportunity.

Repentance is Jesus' exclamation point. "Time's up! Wake up!" It is as if Jesus is saying, "Quit sleepwalking through life!" It is a jarring word and is meant to be so.

Repentance literally means "Rethink your thinking!" The kingdom of darkness has shaped your thinking and is leading you in the wrong direction. You are now entering a "contrast society." The kingdom of God is based on an entirely different set of values. Jesus says, "My kingdom will turn you right side up in an upside-down world."

In other words, *repent* means to make a U-turn. When we enter Jesus' kingdom we are called to a new order of life. Through confession of sin we acknowledge we have been heading in the wrong direction. Disaster awaits. Pull yourself back from the precipice. Now, start a new life that will take a lifetime, for *discipleship* means to engage in the lifelong process of dying to self so that King Jesus can establish his rule in all dimensions of our existence.

Believe the good news. Jesus concludes his presentation of the gospel with "believe the good news." The good news is that we have wondrous new standing with God through Christ. Our sin, which separates us from the holy God, has been forgiven, and our forever future is secure. Yet in our simplistic understanding of salvation we have tended to trivialize the gospel into easy believism. John Ortberg says that in the tradition in which he grew up, people often asked each other, "Have you trusted Christ?" This was code language for "Have you prayed the prayer? Do you believe in an arrangement that has been made for you to get you into heaven when you die?"[4]

But Jesus means far more than praying a formulaic prayer or assenting to set of core beliefs, such as a creed. To believe the good news is active. We need to *live* the good news, which is the kingdom of God. Put your trust in, lean into, place your weight on King Jesus. James Dunn sums it up, "So when Jesus called for belief we can be confident that he had in mind not simply assent in the form of words, or passive expression of trust, but a reliance on God which would become the basis and motivating center for all conduct and relationship."[5]

Conclusion. Can someone be a Christian without being a disciple? Or can we just use Jesus to get into heaven when we die but not live for him during our earthly days? That whole concept is foreign to the New Testament. For Jesus, Paul and Peter there was not a sliver of daylight between being a Christian and a disciple.

Jesus preached the good news of the kingdom of God. The exiled King has arrived. As C. S. Lewis puts it in *The Lion, the Witch, and the Wardrobe*, Aslan, the lion and Christ figure, is "on the move." The White Witch, who ruled Narnia, is losing her power. The icy land of Narnia, where it is always winter but never Christmas, is melting, and spring is in the air. The kingdom of God is penetrating the kingdom of darkness. They are on a collision course. You must choose sides. There is no middle ground. You can't be a Christian without being a disciple.

Core commitments of disciples. So what are we preachers calling people to be and do in response to the good news? What do the beginning stages of discipleship look like for those who are entering the kingdom of God?

The following are the core commitments people should consider if they want to be Christ-followers.

Disciples join Jesus' life. A Christian is "in Christ" and has "Christ in" him or her. Jesus says that we are like branches attached to the vine life flows from (John 15:1-8). The apostle Paul picks up on this agrarian image, saying, "If we have been united with him in a death like his, we will certainly also be united with him in a resurrection like his" (Romans 6:5). The word *united* literally means "engrafted." We are like branches cut from one vine and grafted into another. It is only as we remain in, stay connected to, the vine that we have life. Life flows only in one direction: from the vine to the branches. The branches have no life in themselves apart from the vine. A disciple understands first and foremost that "apart from [him] you can do nothing" (John 15:5).

Disciples join Jesus' community. Being engrafted means in part to become an integral part of the body of Christ. The New Testament knows nothing about individual or solo salvation. We are saved into a new community Jesus has invested his life in. The image of the church as Christ's body is far more than a nice metaphor or word picture. Jesus quite literally continues to live out his life on earth through his replacement people. Just as there is no life apart from our attachment to him, there is no discipleship apart from his community. One vital way we express our connection to the body is to be a part of a microgroup whose members are seeking to become all that Jesus intended.

Disciples join Jesus' mission. Simply put, Jesus' mission is to make disciples. This means that we have to see our identity—in all we are and do—through the lens of being a disciple of Jesus. In other words, our vocation or calling, which undergirds every role we have in life, is to see ourselves as a Jesus follower. We answer the question "Who are you?" with "I am a follower of Jesus." As Jesus' followers our mission is to make more and better disciples. This entails doing all we can to be equipped for this mission.

Thus, disciple making starts with proclamation of the gospel of Jesus, which has a direct and inseparable connection to discipleship.

Preach the Terms of Discipleship

This leads us back to the woman's question: "Why do I have to be a disciple?" One of the playful moments I enjoy when I do workshops on disciple making is to wave my hand over the attendees and proclaim them ordained for the next five minutes. They get to put themselves in the position of being the pastor who must answer this woman's question. Usually someone will get to the point in a blunt manner: "I would tell her she has to be a disciple, because she has no other option. This is not an either-or test. Jesus does not say, Would you like to be a Christian or a disciple? Sorry there aren't two categories. We have made that up."

In other words we have to name the elephant in the room. First, we will note that there are only three times that the word *Christian* appears in the New Testament. Two of those uses are found on the lips of outsiders. We read in Acts 11:26, "It was in Antioch that the disciples were first called 'Christians.'" Many believe that the term *Christian* was derogatory or even a political label for those who were in the "Christ party." Regardless of the intent of the term, note that *disciples* and *Christians* are interchangeable terms. The second use of *Christian* appears in Acts 26:28 in response to the apostle Paul's defense of his faith before King Agrippa II, "Do you think in such a short time you can persuade me to be a Christian?" (NIV). Agrippa was aware that if he accepted the gospel, he would have to associate with a new subculture of Christians. To be a

Christian would require a new way of life in association with a new people. The final use of *Christian* is in the context of being a part of a persecuted minority. "If any of you suffers as a Christian, do not consider it a disgrace, but glorify God because you bear this name" (1 Peter 4:16). The very thing that our woman in question was trying to avoid by using the label Christian is what put people in hot water in Jesus' day. From this brief survey we can see that biblically there is no difference between *Christian* and *disciple*. It is a distinction we have created to accommodate a cheap-grace theology.

The New Testament is a book about discipleship and spiritual formation. In the first five books of the New Testament there are 268 references to disciple(s). Post-Pentecost, the images shift from being a follower to the internal dwelling of Christ through the Holy Spirit. Both point to the ultimate goal of the Christian life: "to be conformed to the image of his Son" (Romans 8:29). In all-encompassing, comprehensive terms Jesus lays out the expectations for any who would follow him: "If any want to become my followers, let them deny themselves and take up their cross daily and follow me" (Luke 9:23). The role of the preacher is to restate without apology or dilution the terms Jesus uses as he lays claim to our lives.

Want to know what it means to deny yourself, take up your cross and lose your life for his sake? Look at the application of these concepts in real-life situations. For example, James and John approached Jesus on the sly with a request to sit on his right and left when he came into his kingdom. Their notion of the kingdom was that Jesus, the Messiah, would soon usher in the kingdom of God through power. Their view of self-importance and personal value meant they wanted to be as close to the center of power as possible. "Look where we sit!" they wanted to say. Jesus flipped their view of power on its head. He said they had been captured by the world's view of power, not his. "You know that among the Gentiles those whom they recognize as their rulers lord it over them, and their great ones are tyrants over them. But it is not so among you" (Mark 10:42-43). If you want to be great in Jesus' kingdom, kneeling before others is the appropriate posture. The King never expects anything from his followers that he has not modeled himself. "The Son of Man

came not to be served but to serve, and to give his life a ransom for many"
(Mark 10:45). This is Jesus' commentary on Luke 9:23.

Our call as preachers is to lay out the cost and the contrast of discipleship. In *The Cost of Discipleship* Dietrich Bonhoeffer said we have
succumbed to *cheap grace*, which I have associated with the term *Christian*,
as it is commonly used. Costly grace, because of the price Jesus paid, is
biblical discipleship. Bonhoeffer said, "When Christ calls a person, he
bids him come and die."[6] Our responsibility as preachers is to live the
call and declare the same.

Preach Discipleship to Preach for Decisions

Repent is a crisis word. It requires a transformation of our thinking.
People are called to take the journey of discipleship by getting out of the
anonymity of the crowd. Just as Jesus selected his apostles from his larger
entourage, even so people must move beyond the noncommitted, those
who are lost in the sea of a congregation. The Christian faith is not a
spectator sport.

So we dare to call people to the next steps of following Christ wherever
they may be. For many (or even most) the next step is to set aside time to
meet weekly with others for the distinct purpose of considering the nature
of discipleship. This will require preachers to have in my mind how faith
in Christ is to be formed and lived out. This book has pictured microgroups as the incubators for followership. Within these circles we consider
together what it means to be Christ's representative in our home, workplace, significant relationships and neighborhood. For others the next step
may be to understand and embrace God's purpose for their lives, and thus
they become stewards of the gifts and talents God has loaned them.

Preachers in disciple-making churches need to see themselves as more
than careful expositors of God's Word, as important as that is. They are
the vision casters for disciple making, which is backed up with their life
investments as personal disciple makers. They lead the disciple-making
strategy and view preaching as one significant component in this process.

Preaching sets the tone for discipleship. Pastors have both the high
calling and distinct privilege of wrestling with the ultimate loyalties
of God's people. Preaching is not for the faint of heart, because we

will be unmasking idols, messing with people's priorities, and calling parents to be model disciplers of their children, even while we are on the journey with them.

Someone has described the pulpit as the boiler room. To preach discipleship is to stoke the flames, to raise the heat. A story is told of the skeptic David Hume, who was walking in the snow long before daybreak. He was making his way with many others to hear the revivalist preacher George Whitefield. Someone said to Hume, "Mr. Hume, I didn't think you believed this message!" He is said to have responded, "I don't, but that man in the chapel does, and I can't stay away!" Winston Churchill sums up my admonition regarding urgency and the tone setting of preaching discipleship. "If you have an important point to make, don't try to be subtle or clever. Use a pile driver. Hit it once. Then come back and hit it again."[7]

If *the* mission of the church is to make disciples who reproduce, then the congregation should sense that this conviction oozes from every pore of the preacher. If you believe it, so will God's people. The faithful preacher puts before the people the terms of Jesus' call as Jesus stated it. It becomes clear that you can't be a Christian without being a disciple.

ACKNOWLEDGMENTS

No book is the product of one person's mind or life experience. Anything good offered in this resource is a product of a multitude of inputs. I can't thank Don Mathieson enough for coming into my life at a formative turning point, my sophomore year in college. He modeled for me that ministry is the realm of all of God's people, not just the professionals who are "called" or have received professional training. Don was my first discipling mentor whose life message was that impact for the kingdom of God comes through up-close and personal relationships.

My call—not only to disciple others personally but also to help the body of Christ catch a vision of intentional disciple making—was nurtured and birthed by people who believed in me more than I believed in myself.

Darrell Johnson, my dearest friend, who I have shared ministry with on a church staff, said to me in word and deed, "More than anyone I know, you have an understanding of equipping ministry."

I was privileged to be a colleague in ministry with one of the finest people on this planet, Dr. Daniel Meyer, pastor of Christ Church of Oak Brook, Illinois. For ten years we worked shoulder-to-shoulder dreaming, plotting, designing and implementing the vision of a disciple-making church.

In recent years I have been honored to be associated with Camarillo Community Church in California. They made the decision be "all in"— defining the identity of their church around the model I have tried to capture in this book. Ralph Rittenhouse, the recently retired senior pastor of this church, and I have now teamed up to take this vision to as many places around this globe as there is fertile soil through the ministry we are calling the Global Discipleship Initiative (GDI).

The last thirty years of microgroup experiences have given me the joy of sharing life with men ranging in age from twenty to seventy. The best thing I ever did as a pastor was intertwine my life with you. I never felt more like a pastor than when we authentically gathered around God's Word and allowed it to penetrate and shape our souls. Thank you for being in my life.

The staff at InterVarsity Press have provided enormous encouragement, if not at times incisive criticism. Their professional standards have only made, I trust, this product of higher quality. Special thanks go to Cindy Bunch, who saw the benefit of *Discipleship Essentials* back in the late 1990s and has welcomed future projects as they have come along. I could not have had a better editor.

These acknowledgments would be woefully inadequate without mentioning the support from Lily, my dear wife of forty-six years. We have had the joy of being each other's cheerleaders, commending the gifts that each of us evidence. Thank you, my dear, for standing by me, especially during those times I barely came up for air.

APPENDIX 1

Frequently Asked Questions

Should the genders be kept separate or mixed in a discipleship relationship?
Some people might argue that true relational maturity ultimately is the ability of the sexes to understand their differences, but I would argue that in the intimacy of a microgroup it is best to have same-sex groups. Having led a group with two women and groups with married couples, I have found it difficult to be transparent about particular male struggles when women are present. My guess is that the same would be true of women with men. The other concern is the obvious inappropriate bonding that could occur in a cross-sex group of this intimate a nature. It has been well documented historically that in an intense spiritual environment heart wires can get crossed. Spiritual passion can easily cross over to sexual passion.

Why is a triad or quad the right size for a discipleship group? Why is a group of ten not as effective?
I identified four ingredients that converge to make for the transformational environment: relational transparency, the truth of God's Word, life-change accountability, and engaged in our God-given mission (see chap. 8). The small group maximizes the interactive nature of these three ingredients. More people water down the impact of these four elements. Relational transparency built on trust takes longer and becomes more difficult the more people involved. The opportunities to interact over and share insights into God's Word are decreased with greater numbers. With a greater

number of people there is a natural tendency to move away from life-change accountability to measuring accountability by external standards and commitments. Additionally, to affirm or help others discern their call or ministry can be complicated by increased numbers in the group.

What does the leader do if a participant is not following through on the covenant?

One of the reasons for and necessities of a covenant is to empower the leader. Without an explicit covenant the leader has no means for account-ability. Having a written covenant, which serves as a basis for recruiting and convening the microgroup, will minimize this difficulty. It also gives the leader a tool that can be used to call those who have agreed to the covenant back to their stated commitments. In *Discipleship Essentials* there are two built-in opportunities to review and renew the covenant. This process is laid out so that the participants self-assess. People tend to be harder on themselves than their partners might be. Depending on where he or she is in relation to the review of the covenant, a leader might want to wait until the group has an opportunity to self-assess and recommit to the covenant. If the problem seems more urgent, then it would be appro-priate for the leader to ask for one-on-one time with a member of the microgroup. I propose a question such as "It appears that you are having difficulty with [whatever the observed behavior]. Is that right? Is there a way I can be of help?" If the problem continues after offered assistance, then the leader will have to make the hard call and say, "It appears that this is not the right time for you to be in this kind of relationship."

How can we encourage those who are lagging in some aspect of preparation?

This is where the leader can be a model and a coach. For example, I often hear complaints about how difficult it is to memorize Scripture. Some people will use the excuse of age. They say, "I just can't remember things like I used to." Besides not letting them off the hook, you might want to explore some coaching techniques. Putting verses on three-by-five cards and carrying them in your purse or pocket for consistent review can be helpful. Go over suggested ways to prepare the material in the lesson. It is better to take twenty to thirty minutes a day and cover material in bite-size chunks than to cram it all in the night before the group gathers. Talk together as a group about the means and patterns each of you use to get ready for the time together. Keeping a life-change journal can be useful. Record changes in habits, thinking patterns, life direction, understanding of God, or relationships that have come as a result of the discipleship process. This can serve as a wonderful record of the way the Lord is in the process of "making all things new."

Is it necessary that church leaders be on board for a discipleship network to be successful?

If the long-term desire is to have a culture-shaping effect on the life of a church or ministry, the leaders must share the philosophy and lifestyle approach to discipling. The ultimate goal is that the ministry staff and the decision-making leaders would not only adopt the philosophy of discipling but also engage in the practice of people building. That having been said, if you as an individual have a vision for making disciples that is not yet shared by church leaders, that should not stop you from beginning your engagement in disciple making. This can be a quiet ministry that grows within the body. In order not to sow seeds of dissension, I would either seek permission from the pastor(s) or church board, or at the least make them aware of your intention. This then lays the groundwork for a bottom-up change and states your desire to work in concert with church leaders.

What if church leaders have a different approach or structure in place?

Some ministry approaches are antithetical to each other and therefore cannot coexist. This leads us back to the underlying values and philosophy of ministry. Fundamentally, microgroups are based on a belief that there are three necessary ingredients that make for transformation. Microgroups are a means to this deeper end. Transformation or making disciples is not necessarily the intent and practice of many ministries. If the fundamental values are not shared, then the ability to create the conditions necessary for transformation will become unattainable.

How do microgroups fit into the broader structure of small group ministry?

Perhaps the best way to address this question is to consider the various kinds of spaces needed for gathering in a church. In his book *The Search to Belong* Joseph Myers shares a helpful scheme as a prism through which to look at the points of connection. He says that it is helpful for a church to have the following spaces: *public, social, personal* and *intimate. Public* space means that a person has a sense of identification with a church through its main *public* practice, worship. As a people move into a church they might next look for *social* space, where they find "people like me" or who share a common chemistry. The "like me" can be anything from shared interests, common convictions, and or age and stage in life. In larger churches this takes the form of subcongregations or mid-size communities.

Next is *personal* space, which might be a small group, typically comprising eight to twelve persons. Here, people learn to share their life together around the truth of God's Word, and they care for each other without the deeper threat of intimacy. This group size, though, weighs against transparent relationships. Only as people move into microgroups do they find *intimate* space or, as Myers calls it, "naked space." Small groups need to provide both personal and intimate space. Introduction to the value of deeper relationships is often found through the less threatening yet still personal connection of a traditional small group. But the environment of a microgroup allows deeper transformation to occur; it also serves as a vehicle for multiplication.

In other words, different size groups serve different purposes. It is important to be clear about what purpose a group serves and where it fits into our attempts to shape people's lives. In one of my churches we championed the motto that we were "majoring in microgroups." In other words, we were pointing people to the ultimate destination of microgroups.

What is the relationship between intentional disciple making and a perceived leadership deficit?

The lack of prepared leaders is experienced in most congregational settings. I rarely hear that a church has an overabundance of leaders. Yet, I like to say, "We don't have a leadership deficit, we have a disciple-making deficit." I believe that our leadership problem would take care of itself if disciple making became our priority. Just as we say, "Disciples are made, not born," so it is with leaders. We want leaders who are disciples who disciple others. When we bypass the disciple-making stage and recruit people into leadership roles whose hearts and character are not formed in Christ, we will get poor role models. We end up putting people in institutional roles so the management of church programs can go on.

My suggestion is to emphasize a growing network of disciple making. Over time this becomes the farm system from which to recruit and groom future leaders. I urge every church that wants to be a disciple-making congregation to make discipleship, that is, being equipped as a disciple and a disciple maker, a prerequisite for key leadership, including professional staff positions.

APPENDIX 2

Critical Considerations for Growing a
Reproducing Disciple-Making Ministry

Discipleship Must Be a Commitment
Shared by All Core Leadership

If a church is going to become a disciple-making congregation and build
a culture of discipleship, it must be the lifestyle of the core leadership,
starting with the senior or lead pastor. When making disciples is the
mission of a church, we must ask, How are we doing this at XYZ church?
The answer to this question is a commitment to a philosophy of ministry,
which becomes a core tenet of the way you live together. For example, if
you are committed to a certain style of worship (contemporary, traditional, blended, etc.), you would not bring someone on staff who is opposed to the way worship is done. The same is true of disciple making.

To define a church culture—the way you live together—requires a
shared approach, which is a clear trumpet call. If you permit multiple
ways of making disciples or allow each staff person or other key leaders
to adopt their own approach, there is little chance that the mission of
disciple making will become a reality.

Camarillo Community Church was able to go from zero to approximately
150 discipleship groups in five years because all the professional staff and
elders were personally engaged in leading reproducing microgroups.

Making Disciples Is a Prerequisite for Key Leadership Roles

If disciple making is the mission of your church, it follows that the leaders will be products of and investors in the disciple-making process. A natural byproduct of a growing disciple-making network is that you are creating your farm system for future leaders. Leaders in the Christian community are made, not born. I have often titled my disciple-making workshop "Facing a Leadership Shortage? Make Disciples First." We hear complaints about the difficulty of finding leaders for positions, from elders on down. My conviction is that we don't have a leadership problem, we have a lack of commitment to intentional disciple making. Not all disciples are leaders, but all leaders had better be disciples and disciple makers.

Emphasize Repeatedly the Value of Reproduction

Perhaps the hardest value to keep in the forefront is that everyone in a microgroup is being groomed to disciple others. Rick Warren has warned us that we need to restate a vision every twenty-six days.[1] We have vision leak. Perhaps the most important corner to turn in people's self-image is that maturity is not about being an end-user. Disciples disciple. The fifth element in the covenant in *Discipleship Essentials* is that microgroup members "will give serious consideration to" leading their own microgroup after the completion of the current one. Mature disciples reproduce in terms of sharing Christ with others and equipping them to walk alongside others so they can assist fellow disciples to maturity and multiplication. As long as people hold on to the consumer identity, they have not adopted the mission of Jesus. So the value of reproduction must be reinforced every time we "review and renew" the covenant. The goal is that people will not just complete the program by leading one more group but will adopt a lifetime lifestyle of making disciples.

Pray Regularly About Your Next Group Members

Keep the value of multiplication before your group by periodically asking the members who the Lord might want them to invite to join them when they are in the lead position. Just as you might keep a prayer list of those who need to know Christ, you could also keep before your microgroup a list of potential microgroup invitees.

Share Testimonies in Public Worship

Stories of transformation are powerful. People identify with the life-change stories of how God is working in microgroups. It's easy to video these stories, edit them and mix them into the flow of worship. When they are thematically consistent with the morning's message, they can be inserted in the center of the message. The seeds sown can open people up to the process of disciple making. It also reinforces the message that this is how we make disciples here.

Create a Sense That Your Microgroup Is Part of a Bigger Movement

Since the microgroups are small, it is easy to feel that any particular group is isolated and alone. It is important that each group feels a part of the vanguard—something big that God is doing within your community of faith. Toward that end you might try the following: hold regular gatherings of your microgroup participants (announce it publicly); have a regular communiqué (approximately quarterly) that is directed to all the members of the microgroups (share written testimonies, the latest stats on the size of the movement, etc.); put video stories on your website that are three to five minutes in length.

Have a Long-Term Vision

I can't stress strongly enough that you need to be in it for the long haul. We need to fight against every impulse within ourselves toward the quick-fix mentality. We need to take a five-year perspective in order to lay in place the values and practices for becoming a disciple-making church. This means working with your leadership board to redefine success away from the three Bs: buildings, budgets and butts. Only as your leadership board shares the mission of the church to make disciples will they form the buffer needed for the transition. Visualize what it would be like down the road to have a cadre of disciple makers as your ministry partners. Imagine people who have internalized a lifestyle of disciple making and who don't have to be constantly motivated. Wouldn't it be wonderful to lead or be a part of this kind of church?[2]

APPENDIX 3

The Importance of Curriculum

The best way for me to underscore the necessity of a disciple-making curriculum is to state what happens if you don't have it.

If You Don't Have a Curriculum, You Don't Have a Plan

A curriculum's primary purpose is to chart the territory of discipleship we need to cover in order to build a basic foundation for Christian living. Most believers have a hodgepodge of disconnected beliefs and practices about the Christian life. People have garnered bits from sermons and Bible studies, thrown in devotional tidbits, and gathered up truths from things they have read or heard people say. Like pieces of a puzzles, these bits of information are tossed into a box (the brain). A good curriculum connects the puzzle pieces to create a complete picture.

If You Don't Have a Curriculum, You Won't Be Intentional

I have defined *discipling* as "an intentional relationship in which we walk alongside other disciples in order to encourage, equip and challenge one another in love to grow toward maturity in Christ. This includes equipping the disciple to teach others as well."[1] Other words for intentional are *purposeful, deliberate* and *covenantal.* This is the opposite of our usual church experience. Instead of intentional, we tend toward haphazard, random or occasional disciple making. In a covenantal relationship we state our intention to cover the key elements of what needs to be incorporated in the practices, beliefs, character and ministry of a disciple of Jesus.

If You Don't Have a Curriculum, You Don't Have a Transferable Tool

A critical but often missing element in empowering people to disciple others is a teaching tool that creates the disciple-making vision, the territory to cover and how to cover it. If we simply exhort people to disciple others without offering them a curriculum, the chances of a significant number of people taking up the disciple-making challenge is remote. If in the process of being in a discipleship group people have both the opportunity to use the material and to lead others during their initial experience, they are equipped with a tool to employ on behalf of others. Once someone feels comfortable using a tool, they of course can use it creatively. But without the tool, they probably won't implement anything at all.

If You Don't Have a Curriculum, You Won't Have a Sense of Progress

One of the reasons for writing a sequential curriculum was that I had no idea if we were making progress. I was simply making it up when meeting with my groups: Need something on devotional life? Grab an article here or there. Need to cover core doctrine? *Basic Christian*ity by John Stott was my standby. Need to talk about marriage, vocation, parenting or how to witness? Where do I get stuff on this? There was no sense of cohesion, and I left those I was discipling without knowing what territory was important to cover. Were we making progress? How could I tell? At least with a curriculum I knew I was addressing the basics of the Christian life and processing this through the personal life experience of each person involved.

If You Don't Have a Curriculum, You Don't Have a Structure to Define Your Time Together

When people gather for encouragement or as accountability partners, their time together easily degenerates into everyday chitchat. In a discipleship group, personal sharing is balanced with application of biblical content via the curriculum. In my experience it is very easy to allow the relational aspect of the group to overwhelm the need to cover and incorporate vital truths. Having a curriculum pulls us back to what needs to be covered; it is our constant touchstone.

NOTES

Introduction: A Story of Transformation

[1] This curriculum, after years of experimentation, refinement and self-publication, has become *Discipleship Essentials,* expanded edition (Downers Grove, IL: InterVarsity Press, 2007).

[2] Bill Hull, *The Disciple Making Pastor* (Grand Rapids: Revell, 1988), 14.

[3] Over the last century, there has been no shortage of excellent resources that focus on the pattern of disciple making. See A. B. Bruce, *The Training of the Twelve* (Grand Rapids: Kregel, 1971); Robert Coleman, *The Master Plan of Evangelism* (Old Tappan, NJ: Revell, 1963); William Hendriksen, *Disciples Are Made, Not Born* (Colorado Springs: Chariot Victor, 1983); Leroy Eims, *The Lost Art of Disciple Making* (Colorado Springs: NavPress, 1978).

1 The Discipleship Gap

[1] Bruce Wydick, "Does Child Sponsorship Work?" *Christianity Today,* June 2013. For the one organization that allowed itself to be studied, the evidence clearly showed that sponsored children had significant advantages in multiple areas over those who were not sponsored.

[2] This congregational survey was originally sponsored by Willow Creek Community of South Barrington, IL. The REVEAL survey is designed so a church can see a snapshot of its members' core beliefs and practices.

[3] For example, Willow Creek had assumed that when a person who was far from God participated frequently in church activities, this would produce someone who loved God and others. As a matter of fact, they discovered that attendance at ministry programs could not be equated with spiritual growth. They also discovered that fully 25 percent of the total membership (mainly those classified as closest to Christ or who are Christ centered) were stalled or dissatisfied in their spiritual growth and were most likely to consider leaving the church. Willow Creek saw that they needed to transition from trying to be a spiritual parent to

being a spiritual coach. They were taking care of the exploring and the growing-in-Christ folks but leaving the Christ-centered people to themselves. These people needed a spiritual growth coach or mentor.

[4]Max DePree, *Leadership Is an Art* (New York: Bantam Doubleday, 1989), 11.

[5]John Stott, quoted in Roger Steer, *Basic Christian: The Inside Story of John Stott* (Downers Grove, IL: InterVarsity Press, 2009), 267.

[6]Pew Research Center, "America's Changing Religious Landscape," May 12, 2105.

[7]In Barna parlance people are classified "born again" if they can give an affirmative answer to two questions: (1) Have you ever made a personal commitment to Jesus Christ that is still important to you today? (2) When I die I will go to heaven because I have confessed my sins and have accepted Jesus Christ as my Savior. "Evangelicals" in the Barna parlance are a more strict subset of "born again." Only about one-fifth of the "born again" group would qualify as evangelicals. Evangelicals subscribe to seven core doctrinal beliefs in addition to affirmative answers to the two qualifier questions for those who are considered born again.

[8]George Barna, *Maximum Faith: Live Like Jesus* (Ventura, CA: Metaformation, 2011), 29.

[9]Bill Hull, *The Disciple Making Pastor* (Grand Rapids: Revell, 1988), 14.

[10]The marks of discipleship chosen as the framework of self-evaluation certainly could vary by church tradition or denomination. I am attempting to identify areas that most of the Christian community would agree are significant indicators of a follower of Christ.

[11]Scott Thumma and Warren Bird, *The Other 80 Percent: Turning Your Church's Spectators into Active Participants* (San Francisco: Jossey-Bass, 2011). The 80/20 rule is attributed to Vilfredo Pareto, an Italian economist who noticed that 20 percent of the (Italy's) population had 80 percent of the land, and 20 percent generated 80 percent of the revenues.

[12]"Survey Describes the Spiritual Gifts That Christians Say They Have," *Barna*, 2009, www.barna.org/barna-update/faith-spirituality/211-survey-describes-the-spiritual-gifts-that-christians-say-they-have.

[13]Dallas Willard, *The Great Omission* (San Francisco: HarperCollins, 2006), 61.

[14]"The State of Discipleship," *Barna*, 2015, 36.

[15]"Self-Described Christians Dominate America but Wrestle with Four Aspects of Spiritual Depth," *Barna.org*, September 13, 2011, www.barna.org/barna-update/faith-spirituality/524-self-described-christians-dominate-america-but-wrestle-with-four-aspects-of-spiritual-depth#.VsybRn04HIU.

[16]Barna, *Maximum Faith*, 39.

[17]"State of Discipleship," 45.

[18]George Barna, *Growing True Disciples* (Ventura, CA: Issachar Resources, 2000), 11.

[19]Dallas Willard, *The Divine Conspiracy* (San Francisco: Harper, 1998), 315.

[20]Martin Luther, *Three Treatises: An Open Letter to the German Nobility* (Philadelphia: Fortress, 1960), 14-17.

[21]Os Guinness, *The Gravedigger Files* (Downers Grove, IL: InterVarsity Press, 1983), 169.

[22]William Diehl, quoted in R. Paul Stevens, *The Other Six Days: Vocation, Work and Ministry in Biblical Perspective* (Grand Rapids: Eerdmans, 1999), 49.

[23]Albert E. Brumley, "This World Is Not My Home," 1937.

[24]Ron Sider, *The Scandal of the Evangelical Conscience* (Grand Rapids: Baker, 2005), 17.

[25]"State of Discipleship," 14.

[26]Robert Bellah, *Habits of the Heart* (New York: Harper & Row, 1985), 221.

[27]Ray Stedman, *Body Life* (Glendale, CA: Regal, 1972), 37.

[28]David Platt, *Follow Me* (Carol Stream, IL: Tyndale House, 2013), 149.

[29]George Barna, "The State of the Church," 2006, p. 27.

[30]Juan Carlos Ortiz, *Disciple* (Carol Stream, IL: Creation House, 1975), 112.

[31]"State of the Bible 2015," *American Bible Society*, 2015, www.americanbible.org /features/state-of-the-bible-2015.

[32]Kenneth Berding, "The Crisis of Biblical Illiteracy and What We Can Do About It," *Biola*, 2014, http://magazine.biola.edu/article/14-spring/the-crisis-of-biblical -illiteracy.

[33]"Is Evangelism Going Out of Style?" *Barna*, December 17, 2013, www.barna.org /barna-update/faith-spirituality/648-is-evangelism-going-out-of-style.

[34]John P. Kotter, *Leading Change* (Boston: Harvard Business School Press, 1996), 35.

[35]George Barna, "Barna Addresses Four Top Ministry Issues of Church Leaders," *Barna Research Online*, September 25, 2000, www.pdcpastort.com/resources/Four +Top+Ministry+Issues+of+Church+Leaders.doc.

2 The Discipleship Malaise:

[1]C. S. Lewis, *Mere Christianity* (New York: MacMillan, 1952), 169-70.

[2]Greg Ogden, *Unfinished Business: Returning the Ministry to the People of God* (Grand Rapids: Zondervan, 2003), chap. 6. This book was originally published under the title *The New Reformation*.

[3]D. Elton Trueblood, *The Incendiary Fellowship* (New York: Harper & Row, 1967), 41.

[4]Randy Pope, *Insourcing: Bring Discipleship Back to the Local Church* (Grand Rapids: Zondervan, 2103), 86.

[5]It is also an interesting to note that the word translated as "distribution" in verse 1 is identical to the word translated as "ministry" in verse 4. In the other words, waiting on tables is as much a ministry as the more noted ministry done by the apostles.

[6]Trueblood, *Incendiary Fellowship*, 43.

[7]George Barna, *Growing True Disciples* (Ventura, CA: Issachar Resources, 2000), 79.

[8]Ibid.

[9]Ibid.

[10]Dallas Willard, *The Divine Conspiracy* (San Francisco: HarperCollins, 1998), 40.

[11]John Ortberg, "Are You Making Better Christians or More Disciples?" REVEAL 2008, Willow Creek Association Resources, www.willowcreek.com/membership /disciples.

[12]Ibid., xv.

[13]Michael Wilkins, *Following the Master: A Biblical Theology of Discipleship* (Grand Rapids: Zondervan, 1992), 25.

[14]Well-known books by these authors are David Platt, *Radical* (Colorado Springs: Multnomah, 2010); Francis Chan, *Crazy Love* (Colorado Springs: David C. Cook, 2013); Shane Claiborne, *The Irresistible Revolution* (Grand Rapids: Zondervan, 2016); Kyle Idleman, *Not a Fan* (Grand Rapids: Zondervan, 2016).

[15]Kent Carlson and Mike Lueken, *Renovation of the Church: What Happens When a Seeker Church Discovers Spiritual Formation* (Downers Grove, IL: InterVarsity Press, 2011), 33-34, 35.

[16]Dallas Willard, *Renovation of the Heart* (Colorado Springs: NavPress, 2002), 191.

[17]Kenda Creasy Dean, *Almost Christian: What the Faith of Our Teenagers Is Telling the American Church* (Oxford: Oxford University Press, 2010), 14.

[18]Ibid., 30.

[19]"The State of Discipleship," *Barna*, 2015, 67.

[20]Warren, *Purpose-Driven Church*, 109.

[21]For further exploration of combining purpose with process, see Thom S. Rainer and Eric Geiger, *Simple Church* (Nashville: B&H Books, 2011).

[22]George Barna, *Growing True Disciples* (Ventura, CA: Issachar Resources, 2000), 41.

[23]"State of Discipleship," 35.

[24]Joel Arthur Barker, *Future Edge: Discovering the New Paradigms of Success* (New York: HarperCollins, 1992), 136.

[25]"The Eastbourne Consultation Joint Statement on Discipleship," International Consultation on Discipleship, September 24, 1999, www.theintentionaldisciple.com /gpage2.html.

[26]Barna, *Growing True Disciples*, 42.

[27]George Orwell, quoted in Bill Hull, *The Disciple Making Pastor* (Grand Rapids: Revell, 1988), 13.

3 Why Jesus Invested in a Few

[1]A. B. Bruce, *The Training of the Twelve* (Grand Rapids: Kregel, 1971), 11.

[2]Gerhard Kittel, *Theological Dictionary of the New Testament*, ed. and trans. Geoffrey Bromiley (Grand Rapids: Eerdmans, 1967), 4:441.

[3]Lawrence Richards, *Christian Education: Seeking to Become Like Jesus* (Grand Rapids: Zondervan, 1975), 83. Social scientists have identified three stages of social influence that lead to in-depth attitude change. The most superficial change occurs through

compliance. A person conforms or changes because an authority has control over the individual. The second level is imitation, which is the desire to conform because one wants to be like another person. This moves to identification, when there is some emotional involvement with the other person. Finally, internalization means that adopted attitudes and behavior have become intrinsically rewarding.

[4]Alicia Britt Chole, "Purposeful Proximity—Jesus' Model of Mentoring," *Enrichment Journal: A Journal of Pentecostal Ministry* (Spring 2001), enrichment journal.ag.org/200102/062_proximity.cfm.

[5]Bruce, *Training of the Twelve*, 13.

[6]Leroy Eims, *The Lost Art of Disciple Making* (Colorado Springs: NavPress, 1978), 45.

[7]Bruce, *Training of the Twelve*, 13.

[8]Paul M. Zehr and Jim Egli, *Alternative Models of Mennonite Pastoral Formation* (Elkhart, IN: Institute of Mennonite Studies, 1992), 43.

[9]Eugene Peterson, *Traveling Light* (Downers Grove, IL: InterVarsity Press, 1982), 182.

[10]Robert Coleman, *The Master Plan of Evangelism* (Old Tappan, NJ: Revell, 1963), 21.

[11]George Martin, quoted in David Watson, *Called and Committed* (Wheaton, IL: Harold Shaw, 1982), 53.

[12]Coleman, *Master Plan of Evangelism*, 21.

4 Jesus' Preparatory Empowerment Model

[1]Robert Coleman, *The Master Plan of Evangelism* (Old Tappan, NJ: Revell, 1963), 117.

[2]David Watson, *Called and Committed* (Wheaton, IL: Harold Shaw, 1982), 9.

[3]Leighton Ford, *Transforming Leadership* (Downers Grove, IL: InterVarsity Press, 1991), 200.

[4]"Memorandum," *Servant Quarters*, www.servant.org/pa_m.htm.

[5]A. B. Bruce, *The Training of the Twelve* (Grand Rapids: Kregel, 1971), 14.

[6]Ibid.

[7]Martin Luther King Jr., quoted in John Claypool, *Opening Blind Eyes* (Nashville: Abingdon, 1983), 75.

[8]Michael Wilkins, *Following the Master: A Biblical Theology of Discipleship* (Grand Rapids: Zondervan, 1992), 107.

[9]Paul Hersey and Ken Blanchard, *Situational Leadership: A Summary* (Escondido, CA: Center for Leadership Studies, 2000), 2.

[10]Thomas Schirrmacher, "Jesus as Master Educator," *Contra Mundum*, accessed February 9, 2016, www.contra-mundum.org/schirrmacher/educator.pdf.

[11]Coleman, *Master Plan of Evangelism*, 39.

[12]Ibid., 38.

[13]Birger Gerhardsson, *The Origins of the Gospel Tradition* (Philadelphia: Fortress, 1979), 17.

[14]Jesus was not denying that he is good, nor was he humbly refusing to receive such a designation. Jesus' retort was meant to call up short the rich young ruler's casual use of the term *good*, for only God is good.

[15]Coleman, *Master Plan of Evangelism*, 110.

[16]Ibid., 112.

5 Paul's Empowerment Model

[1]There is only one reference to Paul having disciples, but this is not Paul's self-designation. "They [Paul's enemies] were watching the gates day and night so that they might kill him; but his disciples took him by night and let him down through an opening in the wall, lowering him in a basket" (Acts 9:24-25).

[2]I see discipleship and spiritual formation as two sides of the same coin. Discipleship is about following Jesus. Spiritual formation is about the life of Jesus emerging from the inside out.

[3]Jack O. Balswick and Judith K. Balswick, *The Family: A Christian Perspective on the Contemporary Home* (Grand Rapids: Baker, 1991), 94.

[4]Ibid., 108.

[5]Ibid., 105.

[6]F. Hauck, "*ko/pos, kopia/ō*," *Theological Dictionary of the New Testament, Abridged in One Volume*, ed. Geoffrey W. Bromiley (Grand Rapids: Eerdmans, 1985), 453.

[7]Quoted in Linda L. Belleville, *Patterns of Discipleship in the New Testament* (Grand Rapids: Eerdmans, 1996), 121.

[8]C. S. Lewis, *Mere Christianity* (New York: Macmillan, 1952), 189.

[9]L. Douglas DeNike and Norman Tiber, "Neurotic Behavior," *Foundations of Abnormal Psychology* (New York: Holt, Rinehart & Winston, 1968), 355.

[10]Bill Hull, *The Disciple Making Pastor* (Grand Rapids: Revell, 1988), 91.

[11]D. Elton Trueblood, *The Incendiary Fellowship* (New York: Harper & Row, 1967), 43.

[12]Balswick and Balswick, *Family*, 107.

[13]Ibid.

6 Life Investment

[1]Ralph Rittenhouse, retired senior pastor, Camarillo Community Church, Camarillo, California. Used by permission.

[2]Greg Ogden, *Discipleship Essentials: A Guide to Building Your Life in Christ* (Downers Grove, IL: IVP Connect, 1998).

[3]Alicia Britt Chole, "Purposeful Proximity—Jesus' Model of Mentoring," *Enrichment Journal* (Spring 2001), http://enrichmentjournal.ag.org/200102/062_proximity.cfm.

[4]Paul D. Stanley and J. Robert Clinton, *Connecting: The Mentoring Relationships You Need to Succeed in Life* (Colorado Springs: NavPress, 1992), 167.

[5]Dick Wolden, quoted in *Discipleship Bytes*, April 1996. *Discipleship Bytes* is the discipleship newsletter of Saratoga Federated Church, Saratoga, California.

[6]Robert Coleman, *The Master Plan of Evangelism* (Old Tappan, NJ: Revell, 1988), 32.

[7]Ibid.

[8]Waylon Moore, quoted in Billie Hanks Jr., *Discipleship: Great Insights from the Most Experienced Disciple Makers*, ed.. and William A. Shell (Grand Rapids: Zondervan, 1981), 125.

[9]Bill Hull, *The Disciple-Making Church* (Grand Rapids: Revell, 1988), 32.

[10]International Leaders for Discipleship, http://vantagepoint3.org/eastbourne -statement-on-discipleship; emphasis added.

[11]Ogden, *Discipleship Essentials*, 17.

[12]Stanley and Clinton, *Connecting*, 48.

[13]Keith Philips, *The Making of a Disciple* (Old Tappan, NJ: Revell, 1981), 15.

[14]Howard Snyder, *Liberating the Church* (Downers Grove, IL: InterVarsity Press, 1983), 248.

[15]David Platt, *Radical: Taking Back Your Faith from the American Dream* (Colorado Springs: Multnomah Press, 2010), 93.

7 Multiplication: Through the Generations

[1]Gary W. Kuhne, "Follow-up—An Overview," in *Discipleship: The Best Writing from the Most Experienced Disciple Makers* (Grand Rapids: Zondervan, 1981), 117.

[2]Ibid.

[3]Paul Stanley and J. Robert Clinton, *Connecting: The Mentoring Relationships You Need to Succeed in Life* (Colorado Springs: NavPress, 1992), 48.

[4]Keith Phillips, *The Making of a Disciple* (Old Tappan, NJ: Revell, 1981), 15.

8 Transformation: The Four Necessary Ingredients

[1]Charles Swindoll, *Come Before Winter* (Portland, OR: Multnomah, 1985), 91.

[2]Roberta Hestenes, *Using the Bible in Groups* (Philadelphia: Westminster Press, 1983), 96-97.

[3]Gordon McDonald, *Restoring Your Spiritual Passion* (Nashville: Thomas Nelson, 1985), 191.

[4]Bob Buford, *Halftime: Moving from Success to Significance* (Grand Rapids: Zondervan, 2008).

[5]Dietrich Bonhoeffer, *Life Together* (New York: Harper & Row, 1954), 112.

[6]I had led a pilot group with two women in order to model for them how this could be done so that we could get the network growing among the women in our church. This was an exception to my general rule that microgroups can develop transparency more easily if they remain the same gender.

[7]*Discipleship Essentials* (Downers Grove, IL: IVP Connect, 2009), the curriculum I have written, was created in order to give a holistic, sequential picture of the core foundations of a disciple's life.

[8]An unreached or least-reached people is a people group with no indigenous community of believing Christians with adequate numbers and resources to evangelize them. For more on unreached people groups see www.joshuaproject.net.

[9]At the time Dr. Hestenes was associate professor of Christian formation and discipleship at Fuller Theological Seminary.

[10]Ralph Rittenhouse, retired pastor of Camarillo Community Church.

9 Practicalities of Disciple Making

[1]See chapter seven for the working definitions of spiritual guide, coach and sponsor.

[2]One of the benefits of Facebook is getting reacquainted with people you have lost touch with. It is a joy to know that after almost forty years the two men mentioned by Jane are still vibrant followers of Jesus, and one is serving as a pastor.

[3]Randy Pope, *Insourcing: Bringing Discipleship Back to the Local Church* (Grand Rapids: Zondervan, 2013), 133.

[4]Leroy Eims, *The Lost Art of Disciple Making* (Colorado Springs: NavPress, 1978), 45.

[5]Robert Coleman, *The Master Plan of Evangelism* (Old Tappan, NJ: Revell, 1963), 37.

[6]Neil Cole, *Cultivating a Life for God* (Carol Stream, IL: Church Smart Resources, 1999).

[7]William Barclay, *The Letters of Timothy, Titus and Philemon* (Philadelphia: Westminster Press, 1956), 181.

[8]Will Allen Dromgoole, "The Bridge Builder," 1900.

10 The Role of Preaching in Making Disciples

[1]Dallas Willard, *Renovation of the Heart* (Colorado Springs: NavPress, 2002), 245.

[2]Scot McKnight, *The King Jesus Gospel* (Grand Rapids: Zondervan, 2011), 73.

[3]Billy Graham, *Steps to Peace with God* (Wheaton, IL: Good News Publishers, nd.), 4.

[4]John Ortberg, "Are You Making Better Christians or More Disciples?" REVEAL 2008, Willow Creek Association Resources, www.willowcreek.com/membership /disciples.

[5]James Dunn, *Jesus' Call to Discipleship* (Cambridge: Cambridge University Press, 1992), 27.

[6]Dietrich Bonhoeffer, *The Cost of Discipleship* (New York: Macmillan, 1949), 7.

[7]Winston Churchill, "Winston Churchill Quotes," *BrainyQuote*, accessed February 23, 2016, www.brainyquote.com/quotes/quotes/w/winstonchu111314.html.

Appendix 2

[1]Rick Warren, *The Purpose Driven Church* (Grand Rapids: Zondervan, 1995), 111.

[2]Read Kent Carlson and Mike Lueken, *Renovation of the Church* (Downers Grove, IL: IVP Books, 2011), for the story of one church's transformation from a seeker-sensitive to a disciple-making congregation.

Appendix 3

[1]Greg Ogden, *Discipleship Essentials* (Downers Grove, IL: IVP Connect, 2009), 17.

ABOUT THE AUTHOR

Greg Ogden (DMin, Fuller Theological Seminary) recently retired from professional church leadership and now lives out his passion of speaking, teaching and writing about the disciple-making mission of the church. Most recently Greg served as executive pastor of discipleship at Christ Church of Oak Brook in the Chicago western suburbs. He previously held the positions of director of the Doctor of Ministry Program at Fuller Theological Seminary and associate professor of lay equipping and discipleship. His book *Discipleship Essentials* has sold over 250,000 copies and been a major influence on discipleship in the contemporary church.

THE ESSENTIALS SET

Discipleship Essentials
Greg Ogden

978-0-8308-1087-1, paperback, 237 pages

The Essential Commandment
Greg Ogden

978-0-8308-1088-8, paperback, 204 pages

Leadership Essentials
Greg Ogden and Daniel Meyer

978-0-8308-1097-0, paperback, 176 pages

New Testament Essentials
Robbie Fox Castleman

978-0-8308-1052-9, paperback, 151 pages

Old Testament Essentials
Tremper Longman III

978-0-8308-1051-2, paperback, 215 pages

Witness Essentials
Daniel Meyer

978-0-8308-1089-5, paperback, 230 pages

Essential Guide to Becoming a Disciple
Greg Ogden

978-0-8308-1149-6, paperback, 144 pages

Global Discipleship Initiative (GDI) trains, supports, and releases pastors and Christian leaders to establish indigenous, multiplying, disciple-making networks of all God's people, both domestically and internationally.

GDI offers one-day **workshops** and ministry-based **coaching**, as well as more extensive **training** domestically.

For more information, go to
globaldiscipeshipinitiative.org

or contact us directly:
Pastor Ralph Rittenhouse, president, ralph@globaldi.org
Dr. Greg Ogden, chairman of the board, greg@globaldi.org